VEGETARIAN
PASTA

Rose Elliot

VEGETARIAN
PASTA

RANDOM HOUSE

NEW YORK

Library of Congress Cataloging-in-Publication Data
Elliot, Rose.
  Vegetarian pasta/Rose Elliot.
    p. cm.
  Includes index.
  ISBN 0-679-77826-8
  1. COOKERY (PASTA) 2. VEGETARIAN COOKERY. I. TITLE.
TX809.M17E45 1997
  641.8'22–dc21   97-6636

Editor: Mari Roberts
Photographer: Patrice de Villiers
Home Economist: Meg Yansz
Stylist: Penny Markham
Indexer: Susan Bosanko

For HarperCollins*Publishers*
Commissioning Editor: Barbara Dixon
Designer: Paul Calver

Random House website address: http://www.randomhouse.com/

98765432

First U.S. Edition

Typeset in Gill Sans and Goudy
Color reproduction by Colourscan, Singapore
Printed and bound in Spain by
Gráficas Estella, S. A. Navarra.

CONTENTS

● ●

Introduction

During the last few years the growing popularity of vegetarianism and of pasta have gone hand in hand. Things have certainly changed since I was a child when vegetarians were few and far between and pasta meant spaghetti out of a can or macaroni and cheese. And pasta is certainly an excellent food for vegetarians: it provides a starting point for a meal that does not involve having to soak beans or grind nuts, and it is something that we can confidently share with our friends, knowing that they will enjoy the results.

From the nutritional point of view, pasta has much to recommend it. It is what is known as a "complex carbohydrate," one of the group of foods that nutritionists rate highly and urge us to use as the basis of our meals, along with plenty of fresh fruit and vegetables and modest amounts of protein. If the dish does not contain vegetables, I usually serve it with a leafy salad, or start or finish the meal with fresh fruit, because I do believe that one of the secrets of healthy eating is to eat at least the amount of fresh fruit and vegetables recommended by the World Health Organization (14 ounces per day), and preferably more.

For the most part, the recipes in this book do not claim to be authentically Italian, although some of them are. They are mostly dishes that have evolved when I have been cooking for my friends and family, or that other people have made for me, and which have worked well and been enjoyed. I hope that you will like them, and that you will remember that there is always room for your own experimentation too, particularly with something easy like pasta.

With my very best wishes, and happy eating,

Rose Elliot

ROSE ELLIOT

Pasta Basics

Cheap to buy, convenient to store, easy to cook, versatile to use, great to eat, good for you and always increasing in popularity, pasta might truly be described as the food of the twenty-first century.

The range of pasta available is becoming more extensive all the time. In Italy there are literally hundreds of different shapes, often with inspired and imaginative names, such as "elephant's teeth" and "angel's hair," and even "priest stranglers." The name by which a pasta shape is known often varies from region to region: this is confusing, but it is also one of the charms of cooking with Italian pasta.

Each shape of pasta has a subtly different role to play and real pasta aficionados take great care in matching the pasta to the right sauce. An Italian might say that this is an innate skill that is difficult for a non-Italian to learn. However, as you experiment with different shapes and sauces, you will develop an instinct for matching pasta and sauce, at least to your own taste. I firmly believe that part of the joy of cooking lies in feeling relaxed and confident enough to try different flavors and combinations for yourself without feeling worried about what is "right" and "wrong." Here are some basic guidelines to help you when making your choice of pasta.

CHOOSING PASTA

Long pastas, such as spaghetti, work best with smooth sauces that will cling to them; a sauce with chunky pieces is difficult to eat with long, slippery strands. The exception to this rule is the long fusilli pasta (fusilli lunghi), a long, coiled pasta that catches chunky pieces in its curls.

Ribbon pastas, which include tagliatelle, pappardelle and fettuccine, are delicate and porous. They are good with creamy sauces, although pappardelle, being so wide, is complemented by strong flavors.

Short tubes, such as penne and rigatoni, are adaptable. These are perhaps the best "all-around" pastas and go well with a number of different sauces, including cream ones. They trap the sauce in their cavities, making it easy to eat, and they are also good with chunky ingredients.

Special shapes, such as conchiglie (shells), fusilli (spirals), farfalle (butterflies or bowties), lumache (snails) and so on, are also perfect for mixing with chunky ingredients and great in pasta salads. Remember that the pasta called gnocchi is named after the small potato dumpling whose shape it copies; if you ask for gnocchi you may get potato dumplings instead. (You need to ask for the pasta version.)

Soup pastas are tiny and include many pretty shapes, such as stellette (little stars), farfalline (baby butterflies), alfabetini (little letters of the alphabet) and orzo, which look like grains of rice.

As well as the Italian pastas, there are also oriental noodles. I have included a couple of recipes using these, concentrating on the ones that are widely available. They are prepared differently from Italian pasta, requiring only a soaking in boiling water before use. Like pasta, they are good for quickly turning a stir-fry or soup into a more substantial dish.

Pasta is now available in flavors, such as beet, saffron, truffle, tomato and basil, as well as the familiar spinach, which creates pasta verde or green pasta. These pastas look beautiful, especially before they are cooked, but, with the exception of spinach pasta, their flavor does not contribute anything to the dish, and they are not used in Italy.

Pasta is made from wheat, but if you cannot eat wheat, or prefer not to, try corn and rice pastas. These are available in colored and flavored versions, which seem to be more successful than those of their wheat counterpart. Corn and rice pastas are available from health food stores or by mail order. Some of them taste surprisingly good. Careful cooking is required: they go from hard to soggy in a matter of moments and I find that they take far less time to cook than is suggested on the packaging.

FRESH OR DRIED PASTA?

Fresh pasta is widely available, but unless it is made on the spot by a skilled pasta-maker and purchased freshly made, it often turns out heavy and disappointing. Pasta does not take kindly to being refrigerated; drying is a far better way of preserving it, which is why, generally, dried pasta is a far better buy than so-called "fresh," and the more you pay for the dried pasta, usually, the better it is.

Stuffed pasta, such as ravioli, tortellini and cappelletti, have to be bought fresh but here again you need to be selective – some of them can be very heavy. I have not included recipes for using these pastas because they are best served simply with butter or olive oil and crushed garlic or chopped herbs, or else with a light sauce, such as fresh tomato.

COOKING PASTA

Allow roughly 3½ ounces of pasta for each person. For every 3½ ounces allow 1 quart of water and ¾ teaspoon of salt when cooking. So you will need:

For 2 people
7 ounces pasta, 2 quarts of water, 1½ teaspoons of salt

For 4 people
14 ounces pasta, 4 quarts of water, 3 teaspoons (1 tablespoon) of salt

Use a large saucepan so that the pasta can move around as it cooks. First bring the saucepan of water to a boil, then add the pasta along with the salt. Cover the pot briefly, then, when the water comes back to the boil (this happens quickly), remove the lid and let the pasta continue at a rolling boil until it is "al dente" – just tender but with a firm bite. This may take less time than that stated on the package, so start testing, by lifting out a piece of pasta and biting it, in good time. It will be hot, so blow on it first! In the recipes in this book I have mostly given an average time of 8 minutes, but you should always use your own judgment and always test the pasta.

When the pasta is done, tip it into a colander set in the sink and shake it gently to remove excess water. You do not need to get the pasta dry, indeed it is better to leave some water still clinging to it. Then you can either put the pasta into a large warmed serving bowl with some olive oil and any other ingredients you are using, or you can do as I do and tip it back into the still-warm saucepan before adding the olive oil and any other additions and tossing it well.

Either way, quickly put the pasta onto warmed plates – pasta cools down rapidly – add toppings if you are using any and serve immediately, *presto*, *pronto* and *buon appetito*!

Fusilli bucati

Lasagnette

Ruote di carro

Pappardelle

There are hundreds of different pasta shapes and some of them have several names that vary in Italy from area to area. So putting a name to a shape can be a little confusing; however, you can often substitute another similar pasta shape in a recipe if necessary. In this book I have used pasta that is quite widely available so finding a particular variety should not pose too many problems. Here and on the next two pages are shown the pasta shapes which are used in the recipes; if you cannot find exactly the type, at least you will know roughly what you are looking for and will be able to buy something similar! I have always found Italian specialty shops very helpful in tracking down particular types of pasta or suggesting alternatives, and it is always fun to try something new.

Pastine **Farfalline**

Egg noodles

Quick Guide to Pasta
•

Stellette

**Lumache
rigate
grandi**

Spaghettini

Fusilli

Nidi vermicelli

Macaroni

Lasagne

Fettuccine

Pipe rigate

Penne rigate

Orecchiette

Farfalle

Nidi
tagliatelle

Pennoni

Gnocchi

Penne

Rigatoni

Spaghetti

Conchiglie
rigate

Pasta Soups

Almost any soup can be made more filling and nutritious with the addition of a handful of pasta. You do not need a great deal: 2–4 ounces for a soup to serve four people is ample. It is a great way of turning a simple soup into a main course.

Tiny soup pastas come in many different shapes and it is fun to try different ones. Children particularly enjoy finding interesting pasta shapes in their food, and a vegetable soup with pasta in it and perhaps a little grated cheese over the top can be a great way to tempt fussy eaters or vegetable-haters.

There are a number of thick and filling soups in this section: Provençal pistou, Tuscan white bean and pasta soup with garlic croutons and Middle Eastern spiced lentil and pasta soup, for instance. Serve with bread and perhaps a side salad as a satisfying main course.

A pasta soup can also be light and delicate, and make an excellent first course. Leek, parsley and pasta broth, Thai coconut soup with noodles, and Fresh tomato soup with farfalline and basil come into this category; they are refreshing and ideal to whet your appetite.

Some of these soups call for stock and, of course, homemade is best if you have it. Otherwise buy a good stock from the supermarket, a good-quality vegetable (vegetarian) stock cube or (my favorite) Swiss vegetable bouillon powder.

HARVEST VEGETABLE AND PASTA SOUP Serves ❹

INGREDIENTS

3 Tbs olive oil

1 onion, peeled and chopped

1 garlic clove, peeled and crushed

1 pound peeled and de-seeded pumpkin, diced

8 ounces carrots, scraped and cut into ¼ inch slices

1 cup corn kernels, cut from the cob, or frozen

5 cups vegetable stock

8 ounces zucchini, trimmed and cut into ¼ inch slices

½ cup small pasta shapes

salt and freshly ground black pepper

4 Tbs roughly chopped fresh parsley, preferably flat-leaf, to serve

This soup makes the most of the late summer harvest of corn and pumpkin, to produce a gloriously golden soup made more substantial with the addition of some pasta. Hot crunchy garlic or herb bread goes well with it or you could serve it with chunks of whole wheat bread and some grated cheese – either a strongly flavored vegetarian Cheddar or freshly grated Parmesan cheese.

1 Heat the oil in a large saucepan and put in the onion, garlic, pumpkin and carrots. Stir briefly, then cover and leave to cook gently for 10–15 minutes, until the vegetables start to become soft.

2 Add the corn kernels and the stock to the pan. Bring to a boil, then lower the heat and leave to simmer over low heat for about 20 minutes.

3 Add the zucchini to the soup, bring back to a boil and simmer for 5 minutes. Then add the pasta and cook for a further 8 minutes.

4 Season the soup with salt and pepper, then serve in warm bowls and top each with plenty of parsley.

TUSCAN WHITE BEAN AND PASTA SOUP WITH GARLIC CROUTONS Serves ❹

INGREDIENTS

olive oil

1 onion, peeled and chopped

2 garlic cloves, peeled and crushed

2 14-ounce cans cannellini beans

5 cups vegetable stock

4 thick slices of bread, crusts removed

½ cup small pasta shapes

salt and freshly ground black pepper

So simple and easy, yet filling and good to eat. The crunchy garlic croutons make a nice touch, but if you have not time to do them, just serve the soup with chunks of bread.

1 Heat 2 tablespoons of olive oil in a large saucepan, put in the onion and half the garlic, stir briefly, then cover and leave to cook gently for 10 minutes, until the onion becomes soft.

2 Add the beans together with their liquid and the stock. Bring to a boil, then lower the heat and leave to simmer for 20 minutes.

3 Meanwhile, make the croutons. Rub the surface of the bread with the remaining garlic, then pan-fry the bread on both sides in a little hot olive oil, until crisp and golden. Cut into small squares and keep on one side.

4 Add the pasta shapes to the soup, bring back to a boil and simmer for 6–8 minutes until the pasta is cooked. Season with salt and pepper, then serve in warm bowls and top each with some croutons.

MIDDLE EASTERN SPICED LENTIL AND PASTA SOUP Serves ❹

INGREDIENTS

3 Tbs olive oil

2 onions, peeled and chopped

2 garlic cloves, peeled and crushed

⅔ cup split red lentils

5 cups vegetable stock

½ cup small pasta shapes

1 Tbs ground coriander

1 Tbs ground cumin

squeeze of lemon juice

salt and freshly ground black pepper

4 Tbs roughly chopped fresh cilantro, to serve

Tasty and comforting, this soup is good served with warmed poppadums or other Indian breads.

1 Heat the oil in a large saucepan, put in the onions and garlic, stir briefly, then cover and leave to cook gently for 10 minutes, until the onions become soft. Transfer about a third of the mixture to a smaller saucepan and leave on one side for the moment.

2 Add the lentils and the stock to the onions in the large saucepan. Bring to a boil, then lower the heat and leave to simmer for 30 minutes. Add the pasta and cook for a further 8 minutes.

3 Meanwhile, reheat the onions and garlic in the smaller saucepan, then stir in the coriander and cumin. Cook for 1 minute, stirring, then remove from the heat and add to the soup, along with a squeeze of lemon juice and salt and pepper to taste.

4 Serve the soup in warm bowls and top each with a good spoonful of chopped fresh cilantro.

THAI COCONUT SOUP WITH NOODLES Serves ❹

INGREDIENTS

1 stalk of lemon grass, finely chopped

1 inch piece of fresh ginger, grated

1 fresh green chili, de-seeded and finely chopped

1 kaffir lime leaf if available, or a piece of lime rind

scant 2 cups canned coconut milk

2 ounces Chinese egg noodles

8 ounces baby corn, cut into ½ inch pieces

juice of 1 lime

salt and freshly ground black pepper

4–6 Tbs chopped fresh cilantro, to serve

This attractive soup is delicate and creamy, with hot and sour Thai flavorings. I use the kind of noodles that come pressed into a block, but you could also use other thin, quick-cooking varieties.

1 Put the lemon grass, ginger, chili and lime leaf or lime rind into a saucepan with 2½ cups of water. Bring to a boil, then cover and simmer gently for 15 minutes, for the water to absorb the flavors.

2 Next, either scoop out and discard the chopped lemon grass, ginger, chili and lime leaf or rind, squeezing as much water from them as possible first, or keep them in the soup, depending on your taste – I prefer to keep them in.

3 Add the coconut milk to the pan and bring to a boil, then put in the noodles and corn and cook for a further 2–3 minutes, until the noodles are soft.

4 Add lime juice, and salt and pepper to taste. Serve in warm bowls with a generous sprinkling of chopped fresh cilantro on each.

WOODLAND MUSHROOM AND PASTA SOUP Serves ❹

Assorted wild mushrooms, sometimes sold by the bag in supermarkets, are great for this soup. It is also a wonderful way to celebrate a successful mushroom foray in the woods. Otherwise, make up your own selection of mushrooms from whatever is available, or use all one type – field mushrooms if you can get them, but even regular domestic mushrooms are good.

1 Put the dried porcini mushrooms into a small bowl and cover with ⅔ cup boiling water. Leave for 15–30 minutes to soak. Then drain them, catching and reserving the liquid. Chop the mushrooms.

2 Heat the oil in a large saucepan, put in the onion and garlic, stir briefly, then cover and leave to cook gently for 10 minutes, until the onions start to become soft.

3 Add the fresh mushrooms and the soaked mushrooms to the onions. Stir, then cook, uncovered, for 15 minutes or so until the mushrooms are completely tender.

4 Pour in the stock, then add the reserved mushroom liquid, pouring it through a fine strainer or a piece of cheesecloth to catch any dirt (with the packaged porcini now available it is unusual to find any, but it is best to be on the safe side). Bring to a boil, then lower the heat and leave to simmer for 5 minutes.

5 Put in the pasta and cook for a further 6–8 minutes until done. Then season the soup and serve it in warm bowls with parsley scattered on top of each.

FRESH TOMATO SOUP WITH FARFALLINE AND BASIL Serves ❹

This is a light and refreshing pasta soup that makes the most of the flavor of summer tomatoes, especially if you have plenty in the yard. It is nice for a summer lunch, followed by a garden salad.

1 Heat the oil in a large saucepan, put in the onion and garlic, stir briefly, then cover and leave to cook gently for 10 minutes, until the onions start to become soft.

2 Add the tomatoes, stir, then cover and cook for a further 10–15 minutes, until the tomatoes have collapsed.

3 Add the stock, bring to a boil, then lower the heat and leave to simmer for 5 minutes. Then put in the farfalline and cook for a further 5–8 minutes.

4 Season the soup with salt and pepper to taste, then serve it in warm bowls. Tear some basil leaves over each serving.

LEEK, PARSLEY AND PASTA BROTH Serves ❹

INGREDIENTS

2 Tbs olive oil

1½ pounds leeks, trimmed and cut into ¼ inch slices

1 garlic clove, peeled and crushed

5 cups vegetable stock

⅔ cup small pasta shapes

4–6 Tbs chopped fresh parsley, preferably flat-leaf

salt and freshly ground black pepper

freshly grated Parmesan cheese, to serve

The better the vegetable stock you use for this broth, the better this soup will be. Homemade stock is best if you have time to make it; otherwise, buy good vegetable stock or bouillon powder or concentrate – it is worth trying different brands in small quantities to find your favorite.

1 Heat the oil in a large saucepan and put in the leeks and garlic. Stir briefly, then cover and leave the vegetables to cook gently for 10–15 minutes, until the leeks start to become soft. Stir the contents of the pan from time to time to prevent sticking.

2 Add the stock, stir, then cook for a further 10–15 minutes. Add the pasta, bring to a boil and cook for 8–10 minutes more.

3 Stir in the parsley, season with salt and pepper, then serve in warm bowls and hand around the Parmesan.

SUMMER GARDEN PASTA SOUP WITH FRESH HERBS Serves ❹

INGREDIENTS

2 Tbs olive oil

1 onion, peeled and chopped

1 garlic clove, peeled and crushed

8 ounces young carrots, thinly sliced

5 cups vegetable stock

¾ cup shelled fresh peas

⅔ cup shelled fresh fava beans

1¼ cups young green beans, cut into 1-inch lengths

4 ounces zucchini, trimmed and thinly sliced

½ cup small pasta shapes

salt and freshly ground black pepper

4 Tbs chopped fresh herbs: parsley, chives and mint

freshly grated Parmesan cheese, to serve

Easy and quick to do, this makes an effortless light meal for an early summer day. You can vary the vegetables according to what is available. Serve it with warmed bread or rolls or hot garlic bread and maybe a glass of chilled white wine. Complete the seasonal meal with some summer fruits, simply prepared: black cherries, strawberries or raspberries with some thick-set yogurt or crème fraîche if you like, or a make-ahead gooseberry fool.

1 Heat the oil in a large saucepan, put in the onion, garlic and carrots, stir briefly, then cover and leave to cook gently for 10 minutes, until the vegetables start to become soft.

2 Add the stock and bring to a boil over high heat, then add the shelled peas, fava beans, green beans and zucchini. Bring back to a boil, then add the pasta shapes, reduce the heat slightly and cook for about 6–8 minutes, until the vegetables and pasta are cooked.

3 Season with salt and pepper, stir in the herbs, then serve in warm bowls and top each with a good spoonful of Parmesan.

PROVENÇAL PISTOU Serves ❹

INGREDIENTS

3 Tbs olive oil

1 onion, peeled and chopped

1 garlic clove, peeled and crushed

1 leek, trimmed and cut into ¼ inch slices

2 celery stalks, trimmed and chopped

8 ounces carrots, scraped and cut into ¼ inch slices

14 ounces canned chickpeas

5 cups vegetable stock

4 fresh tomatoes, skinned and chopped

1 medium zucchini, trimmed and cut into ¼ inch slices

½ cup small pasta shapes

¼ cup pesto sauce: a good bought one, or see page 76

salt and freshly ground black pepper

freshly grated Parmesan cheese, to serve

There are many versions of this tasty soup from southern France. They are all based on a vegetable soup that includes chickpeas, with pasta and pesto added toward the end of the cooking time. It is a wonderfully hearty, "meal in itself" kind of soup; the only accompaniment it needs is some good bread and perhaps a glass of wine.

1 Heat the oil in a large saucepan, put in the onion, garlic, leek, celery and carrots, stir briefly, then cover and leave to cook gently for 10–15 minutes, until the vegetables start to become soft.

2 Add the chickpeas together with their liquid and the stock. Bring to a boil, then lower the heat and leave to simmer for 20 minutes.

3 Add the tomatoes and zucchini to the soup, bring back to a boil and simmer for 5 minutes. Then add the pasta and cook for a further 10 minutes.

4 Stir in the pesto sauce, check the seasoning, then serve in warm bowls and top each with a good spoonful of Parmesan.

Pasta Salads

I found this one of the most enjoyable sections of the book to write. I love salads anyway, but I particularly liked having the chance to experiment with different combinations that included pasta. As with soups, when you add pasta to a salad it becomes more filling and turns immediately from a side dish into something more serious. I soon realized that you can add pasta to almost any salad, with good results. Pasta salads are best eaten warm or at room temperature. They can be allowed to get cool, but they are best not refrigerated as the cold air tends to make them heavy.

Pasta salads are good additions to a group of salads for a party; they are useful for serving with a light main course to make a more substantial meal; they make wonderful appetizers, and, as I have said, can be main courses in their own right. If you are serving a pasta salad as a main course, offer warm bread with it, and perhaps another, more simple salad, made from an ingredient that is not included in the pasta salad: tomato, green leaves or grated carrot tossed in vinaigrette with chopped herbs or scallions, for example.

When making salads, use the best flavoring ingredients you can. The better the olive oil and vinegar you use, the better the salad will be, and you only need small amounts. I like to use good-quality extra virgin olive oil and red wine vinegar for salads.

FARFALLE SALAD WITH ASPARAGUS AND NEW PEAS IN MINT VINAIGRETTE Serves ❹

INGREDIENTS

14 ounces farfalle

salt

1 pound asparagus, trimmed and halved to make pieces about 2 inches long

1½ cups shelled fresh peas

3 Tbs olive oil

1 Tbs wine vinegar

freshly ground black pepper

2 Tbs freshly chopped or torn mint

A delicious, refreshing salad for summer, perfect with a glass of chilled white wine.

1 First fill a large saucepan with 4 quarts of water and bring to a boil over high heat for the pasta.

2 When the water boils, add the pasta along with a tablespoon of salt and give the pasta a quick stir. Briefly put the lid on until it starts to lift, showing that the water has come back to a boil, then let the pasta bubble away, uncovered, for about 8 minutes, or until it is tender but still has some bite to it.

3 Meanwhile, cook the asparagus in a little boiling water until just tender: 6–8 minutes. About a minute before it is done, put in the peas. Drain the asparagus and peas.

4 Make a vinaigrette by putting the oil, vinegar and a seasoning of salt and pepper into a jar and shaking until combined.

5 Drain the pasta by tipping it all into a colander placed in the sink, then put it back into the still-warm pan. Add the asparagus, peas and mint. Give the vinaigrette a quick shake, then add to the pasta and stir gently until everything is coated. Serve immediately, or cover and leave until the salad cools to room temperature.

PENNE RIGATE SALAD WITH SUN-DRIED TOMATOES, ARTICHOKE HEARTS, BASIL AND PARMESAN Serves ❹

INGREDIENTS

14 ounces penne rigate

salt

3 Tbs olive oil

1 Tbs wine vinegar

½ tsp Dijon mustard

1 garlic clove, peeled and crushed

freshly ground black pepper

14 ounces canned artichoke hearts, drained and sliced

8 sun-dried tomatoes, chopped

1¼ cups fresh Parmesan cheese, cut in flakes

4 good sprigs of fresh basil, torn

I find canned artichoke hearts useful in pasta dishes – I love their piquant flavor – but you could also use artichokes that have been bottled in oil. In this case, use some of the oil to make the vinaigrette, and go easy on the vinegar, because the flavor may not need much sharpening.

1 First fill a large saucepan with 4 quarts of water and bring to a boil over high heat for the pasta.

2 When the water boils, add the pasta along with a tablespoon of salt and give the pasta a quick stir. Briefly put the lid on until it starts to lift, showing that the water has come back to a boil, then let the pasta bubble away, uncovered, for about 8 minutes, or until it is tender but still has some bite to it.

3 Make a vinaigrette by putting the oil, vinegar, mustard, garlic and a seasoning of salt and pepper into a jar and shaking until thoroughly combined.

4 Drain the pasta by tipping it all into a colander placed in the sink, then put it back into the still-warm pan. Add the artichoke hearts, sun-dried tomatoes, Parmesan and basil. Give the vinaigrette a quick shake, then add to the pasta and stir gently until everything is coated. Serve immediately, or cover and leave until the salad cools to room temperature.

PENNE WITH BROILED MIXED PEPPERS IN SUN-DRIED TOMATO VINAIGRETTE Serves ❹

INGREDIENTS

2 red bell peppers

2 yellow bell peppers

14 ounces penne

salt

3 Tbs olive oil

2 Tbs sun-dried tomato purée

1 Tbs wine vinegar

1 garlic clove, peeled and crushed

freshly ground black pepper

freshly torn basil leaves and flakes of Parmesan cheese, to serve

Vibrant colors and flavors make this a delectable salad served with sourdough rolls.

1 First fill a large saucepan with 4 quarts of water and bring to a boil for the pasta.

2 Next prepare the peppers by cutting them into quarters and placing, skin-side (shiny side) up, on a broiler pan. Put under high heat for 10–15 minutes, until the skin has blistered and blackened in places. Cover the peppers with a plate and leave until cool enough to handle, then remove the skin, stem and seeds, and cut the flesh into strips.

3 When the water in the saucepan boils, add the pasta along with a tablespoon of salt and give the pasta a quick stir. Briefly put the lid on until it starts to lift, showing that the water has come back to a boil, then let the pasta bubble away, uncovered, for about 8 minutes, or until it is tender but still has some bite to it.

4 Make a vinaigrette by putting the oil, sun-dried tomato purée, vinegar, garlic and a seasoning of salt and pepper into a jar and shaking until combined.

5 Drain the pasta by tipping it all into a colander placed in the sink, then put it back into the still-warm pan. Add the peppers. Give the vinaigrette a quick shake, then add it to the pasta and stir gently until everything is coated. Serve immediately, or cover and leave until the salad cools to room temperature. In either case, scatter with the basil and Parmesan before serving.

COLD NOODLE SALAD Serves ❹

INGREDIENTS

14 ounces Chinese noodles

2 Tbs roasted sesame oil

2 Tbs soy sauce

1 Tbs rice vinegar if available

1 garlic clove, peeled and crushed

4 ounces snow peas, trimmed and sliced diagonally

4 ounces baby corn, sliced diagonally

4 scallions, trimmed and sliced

2 Tbs chopped fresh cilantro

salt and freshly ground black pepper

½ cup roasted peanuts, optional

The roasted sesame oil used in this recipe really makes the flavor, and the soft noodles contrast well with the crisp vegetables. If you cannot get rice vinegar, which is delicate and light, use a squeeze of lemon juice instead.

1 Bring a saucepan full of water to a boil. Put the noodles into a large bowl, cover generously with boiling water and leave for 2–3 minutes (or according to the instructions on the package) until tender, then drain.

2 Pour the noodles into a serving bowl and add the roasted sesame oil, soy sauce, rice vinegar and garlic to them. Toss together gently to mix well.

3 Cook the snow peas and corn together in a little boiling water for 1–2 minutes until just tender. Drain, refresh under cold water and drain again.

4 Add the snow peas and corn to the noodles, along with the scallions, cilantro and salt and pepper to taste.

5 Serve immediately, or cover and leave until the salad cools to room temperature. In either case, add the peanuts, if using, just before you serve the salad.

FARFALLE SALAD WITH GRUYÈRE, CHERRY TOMATOES AND SCALLIONS Serves ❹

INGREDIENTS

bunch of scallions, trimmed and cut into long ribbons

14 ounces farfalle

salt

3 Tbs olive oil

1 Tbs wine vinegar

½ tsp Dijon mustard

freshly ground black pepper

8 ounces cherry tomatoes, halved

1 cup Gruyère cheese, diced or coarsely grated

2 Tbs freshly chopped or torn flat-leaf parsley

Serve this salad with soft whole grain rolls or ciabatta bread and a green salad on the side for a complete light meal.

1 First fill a large saucepan with 4 quarts of water and bring to a boil over high heat for the pasta.

2 Meanwhile, put the scallion ribbons into a bowl of ice water and leave on one side to curl.

3 When the water in the saucepan boils, add the pasta along with a tablespoon of salt and give the pasta a quick stir. Briefly put the lid on until it starts to lift, showing that the water has come back to a boil, then let the pasta bubble away, uncovered, for about 8 minutes, or until it is tender but still has some bite to it.

4 Make a vinaigrette by putting the oil, vinegar, mustard and a seasoning of salt and pepper into a jar and shaking until thoroughly combined.

5 Drain the pasta by tipping it all into a colander placed in the sink, then put it back into the still-warm pan. Drain the scallions and add them to the pasta along with the tomatoes, Gruyère and parsley. Give the vinaigrette a quick shake, then add to the pasta and stir gently until everything is coated. Serve immediately, or cover and leave until the salad cools to room temperature.

PENNE RIGATE SALAD WITH MAYONNAISE, CELERY, APPLE AND TOASTED PINE NUTS Serves ❹

INGREDIENTS

⅓ cup raisins

14 ounces penne rigate

salt

2 sweet apples

1 Tbs lemon juice

3 Tbs mayonnaise

3 Tbs plain low-fat yogurt

freshly ground black pepper

1 celery heart, trimmed and sliced

4 scallions, trimmed and chopped

1 cup pine nuts, toasted
(see page 78)

Pasta in creamy mayonnaise with crisp celery, nuts and apples makes a very pleasant salad. It is very good as part of a group of salads for a buffet.

1 First fill a large saucepan with 4 quarts of water and bring to a boil over high heat for the pasta.

2 Meanwhile, put the raisins into a small bowl, cover with boiling water and leave to plump up.

3 When the water in the saucepan boils, add the pasta along with a tablespoon of salt and give the pasta a quick stir. Briefly put the lid on until it starts to lift, showing that the water has come back to a boil, then let the pasta bubble away, uncovered, for about 8 minutes, or until it is tender but still has some bite to it.

4 Cut the apples into small dice or thin slices, removing the core but keeping the skin on. Sprinkle with the lemon juice to preserve the color.

5 Drain the pasta by tipping it all into a colander placed in the sink, then put it back into the still-warm pan. Add the mayonnaise, yogurt and some salt and pepper to taste and stir gently until all the pasta is coated.

6 Drain the raisins and add to the mixture, along with the apples with their lemon juice, the celery and the scallions. Check the seasoning, then serve immediately, or cover and leave until the salad cools to room temperature. Either way, scatter with the toasted pine nuts just before serving.

RUOTE DI CARRO WITH CORN, RED AND GREEN BELL PEPPERS AND CHILI VINAIGRETTE Serves ❹

INGREDIENTS

14 ounces ruote di carro

salt

3 Tbs olive oil

1 Tbs wine vinegar

½ tsp Dijon mustard

1 dried red chili, crumbled

1 garlic clove, peeled and crushed

freshly ground black pepper

1⅓ cups fresh or frozen corn

1 red bell pepper, de-seeded and finely chopped

1 green bell pepper, de-seeded and finely chopped

Fresh raw bell peppers are used in this recipe, giving a crisp texture and refreshing flavor. They combine well with the corn, making this a popular salad with children – who might prefer a not too "hot" version, so just add chili to taste or leave it out. Ruote di carro (cartwheel-shaped pasta) is good for this dish, but if you cannot get it, use another smallish pasta, such as orecchiette or farfalle.

1 First fill a large saucepan with 4 quarts of water and bring to a boil over high heat for the pasta.

2 When the water boils, add the pasta along with a tablespoon of salt and give the pasta a quick stir. Briefly put the lid on until it starts to lift, showing that the water has come back to a boil, then let the pasta bubble away, uncovered, for about 8 minutes, or until it is tender but still has some bite to it.

3 Make a vinaigrette by putting the oil, vinegar, mustard, chili, garlic and a seasoning of salt and pepper into a jar and shaking until combined.

4 A couple of minutes before the pasta is ready, add the corn to the pan – it will only take a minute or two to cook.

5 Drain the pasta and corn by tipping it all into a colander placed in the sink, then put them back into the pan and add the chopped peppers. Give the vinaigrette a quick shake to mix the ingredients, then add to the pasta and stir gently until everything is coated. Serve immediately, or cover and leave until the salad cools to room temperature.

PENNE SALAD WITH RADICCHIO, RED BELL PEPPERS AND BLACK OLIVES Serves ❹

INGREDIENTS

2 red bell peppers

14 ounces penne

salt

3 Tbs olive oil

1 Tbs wine vinegar

½ tsp Dijon mustard

1 garlic clove, peeled and crushed

freshly ground black pepper

1 small radicchio, shredded or torn

⅓ cup black olives

This is a lovely salad for autumn, with sweet, succulent broiled red peppers contrasting with bitter-tasting radicchio leaves and salty black olives.

1 First fill a large saucepan with 4 quarts of water and bring to a boil over high heat for the pasta.

2 Next prepare the peppers by cutting them into quarters and placing, skin-side (shiny side) up, on a broiler pan. Put under high heat for 10–15 minutes, until the skin has blistered and blackened in places. Cover the peppers with a plate and leave until cool enough to handle, then remove the skin, stem and seeds, and cut the flesh into strips.

3 When the water in the saucepan boils, add the pasta along with a tablespoon of salt and give the pasta a quick stir. Briefly put the lid on until it starts to lift, showing that the water has come back to a boil, then let the pasta bubble away, uncovered, for about 8 minutes, or until it is tender but still has some bite to it.

4 Make a vinaigrette by putting the oil, vinegar, mustard, garlic and a seasoning of salt and pepper into a jar and shaking until combined.

5 Drain the pasta by tipping it all into a colander placed in the sink, then put it back into the still-warm pan. Add the red pepper strips, radicchio and olives. Give the vinaigrette a quick shake, then add to the pasta and stir gently until everything is coated. Serve immediately, or cover and leave until the salad cools to room temperature.

PENNE RIGATE SALAD WITH BROCCOLI AND CHERRY TOMATOES Serves ❹

INGREDIENTS

14 ounces penne rigate

salt

8 ounces broccoli, divided into small florets, tough stems removed and tender stems chopped

3 Tbs olive oil

1 Tbs wine vinegar

½ tsp Dijon mustard

1 garlic clove, peeled and crushed

freshly ground black pepper

8 ounces cherry tomatoes, halved

2–3 good sprigs of basil, freshly torn or shredded

The combination of white pasta with green broccoli and red cherry tomatoes makes this a particularly good salad for a Christmas meal, giving a festive look to the table – but it is delicious any time of the year.

1 First fill a large saucepan with 4 quarts of water and bring to a boil over high heat for the pasta.

2 When the water boils, add the pasta along with a tablespoon of salt and give the pasta a quick stir. Briefly put the lid on until it starts to lift, showing that the water has come back to a boil, then let the pasta bubble away, uncovered, for about 8 minutes, or until it is tender but still has some bite to it.

3 Meanwhile, cook the broccoli in a little boiling water for 3–4 minutes until tender. Drain the broccoli.

4 Make a vinaigrette by putting the oil, vinegar, mustard, garlic and a seasoning of salt and pepper into a jar and shaking until combined.

5 Drain the pasta by tipping it all into a colander placed in the sink, then put it back into the still-warm pan. Add the broccoli, cherry tomatoes and basil. Give the vinaigrette a quick shake, then add to the pasta and stir gently until everything is coated. Serve immediately, or cover and leave until the salad cools to room temperature.

FUSILLI SALAD WITH COTTAGE CHEESE, CHERRY TOMATOES AND CHIVES IN LEMON VINAIGRETTE Serves ❹

INGREDIENTS

14 ounces fusilli

salt

3 Tbs olive oil

1 Tbs lemon juice

finely grated or thinly pared rind of ½–1 lemon

½ tsp Dijon mustard

1 garlic clove, peeled and crushed

freshly ground black pepper

1 cup cottage cheese

8 ounces cherry tomatoes, halved

2 Tbs freshly chopped chives

A perfect light salad for summer. Use a zester to make the lemon strands if you have one; otherwise grate the lemon rind finely, or peel thinly and then chop into strands.

1 First fill a large saucepan with 4 quarts of water and bring to a boil over high heat for the pasta.

2 When the water boils, add the pasta along with a tablespoon of salt and give the pasta a quick stir. Briefly put the lid on until it starts to lift, showing that the water has come back to a boil, then let the pasta bubble away, uncovered, for about 8 minutes, or until it is tender but still has some bite to it.

3 Make a vinaigrette by putting the oil, lemon juice and rind, mustard, garlic and a seasoning of salt and pepper into a jar and shaking until combined.

4 Drain the pasta by tipping it all into a colander placed in the sink, then put it back into the still-warm pan. Add the cottage cheese, breaking it up roughly with a fork so that it is in lumps rather than finely distributed, together with the cherry tomatoes and chives. Give the vinaigrette a quick shake, then add to the pasta and stir gently until everything is coated. Serve immediately, or cover and leave until the salad cools to room temperature.

SALADE NIÇOISE WITH CONCHIGLIE Serves ❹

INGREDIENTS

14 ounces conchiglie

salt

3 Tbs olive oil

1 Tbs wine vinegar

½ tsp Dijon mustard

1 garlic clove, peeled and crushed

freshly ground black pepper

4 tomatoes, preferably plum, roughly chopped

4 hard-boiled eggs, shelled and sliced

bunch of scallions, trimmed and chopped

⅓ cup black olives

2 Tbs freshly chopped or torn flat-leaf parsley

Adding pasta to a vegetarian salade niçoise results in a lovely, substantial mixture that makes an excellent main course.

1 First fill a large saucepan with 4 quarts of water and bring to a boil over high heat for the pasta.

2 When the water boils, add the pasta along with a tablespoon of salt and give the pasta a quick stir. Briefly put the lid on until it starts to lift, showing that the water has come back to a boil. Then let the pasta bubble away, uncovered, for about 8 minutes, or until it is tender but still has some bite to it.

3 Make a vinaigrette by putting the oil, vinegar, mustard, garlic and a seasoning of salt and pepper into a jar and shaking until combined.

4 Drain the pasta by tipping it all into a colander placed in the sink, then put it back into the still-warm pan. Add the tomatoes, hard-boiled eggs, scallions, black olives and parsley. Give the vinaigrette a quick shake, then add to the pasta and stir gently until everything is coated. Serve the pasta salad immediately, or cover the bowl and leave it until the salad has cooled to room temperature.

GNOCCHI, AVOCADO AND TOMATO SALAD WITH BASIL VINAIGRETTE Serves ❹

INGREDIENTS

14 ounces gnocchi

salt

3 Tbs olive oil

1 Tbs wine vinegar

½ tsp Dijon mustard

1 garlic clove, peeled and crushed

freshly ground black pepper

1 pound tomatoes, sliced

2–3 good sprigs of basil, torn or shredded

1 avocado

juice of ½ lemon

This salad can be made in advance and allowed to get cool, but, if you do so, add the avocado at the last moment so that it keeps its bright color.

1 First fill a large saucepan with 4 quarts of water and bring to a boil over high heat for the pasta.

2 When the water boils, add the pasta along with a tablespoon of salt and give the pasta a quick stir. Briefly put the lid on until it starts to lift, showing that the water has come back to a boil. Then let the pasta bubble away, uncovered, for about 8 minutes, or until it is tender but still has some bite to it.

3 Make a vinaigrette by putting the oil, vinegar, mustard, garlic and a seasoning of salt and pepper into a jar and shaking until the ingredients are combined.

4 Drain the pasta by tipping it all into a colander placed in the sink, then put it back into the still-warm pan. Give the vinaigrette a quick shake, then add to the pasta and stir gently until the pasta is coated.

5 Allow to cool, then add the tomatoes and basil. Just before serving, halve the avocado, remove the pit and skin and slice the flesh. Sprinkle with lemon juice and salt and pepper and add to the salad. Toss gently, then serve.

Salade niçoise with conchiglie

CONCHIGLIE SALAD WITH FENNEL, TOMATOES AND OLIVES Serves ❹

INGREDIENTS

14 ounces conchiglie

salt

3 Tbs olive oil

1 Tbs wine vinegar

½ tsp Dijon mustard

1 garlic clove, peeled and crushed

freshly ground black pepper

1 large fennel

1 pound tomatoes, preferably plum, roughly chopped

⅔ cup black olives

Fennel, with its crunchy texture and aniseed flavor, makes a refreshing ingredient in this salad, but you could use a celery heart instead.

1 First fill a large saucepan with 4 quarts of water and bring to a boil over high heat for the pasta.

2 When the water boils, add the pasta along with a tablespoon of salt and give the pasta a quick stir. Briefly put the lid on until it starts to lift, showing that the water has come back to a boil, then let the pasta bubble away, uncovered, for about 8 minutes, or until it is tender but still has some bite to it.

3 Make a vinaigrette by putting the oil, vinegar, mustard, garlic and salt and pepper into a jar and shaking until combined.

4 Cut any leafy bits off the fennel, chop them roughly and leave them on one side. With a sharp knife pare from the fennel any tough, stringy outer layers, then dice or chop the flesh.

5 Drain the pasta by tipping it all into a colander placed in the sink, then put it back into the still-warm pan. Add the fennel, tomatoes and olives. Give the vinaigrette a quick shake, then add to the pasta and stir gently until everything is coated. Scatter the reserved leafy bits of fennel on top. Serve immediately, or cover and leave until the salad cools to room temperature.

FUSILLI SALAD WITH CUCUMBER, DILL MAYONNAISE AND TOASTED ALMONDS Serves ❹

INGREDIENTS

14 ounces fusilli

salt

3 Tbs mayonnaise

3 Tbs plain low-fat yogurt

½ cucumber, cut into ¼ inch dice

4 scallions, trimmed and chopped

2 Tbs freshly chopped dill

freshly ground black pepper

1 cup flaked almonds, toasted (see page 78)

Like the other salads in this book that contain mayonnaise, this salad is dressed with a mixture of mayonnaise and plain yogurt, for a less fatty result. You could add a greater or smaller quantity of yogurt (or none at all) for a lighter or richer result, according to your taste. In any case, this salad is good with some warm, crusty bread.

1 First fill a large saucepan with 4 quarts of water and bring to a boil over high heat for the pasta.

2 When the water boils, add the pasta along with a tablespoon of salt and give the pasta a quick stir. Briefly put the lid on until it starts to lift, showing that the water has come back to a boil, then let the pasta bubble away, uncovered, for about 8 minutes, or until it is tender but still has some bite to it.

3 Drain the pasta by tipping it all into a colander placed in the sink, then put it back into the still-warm pan. Add the mayonnaise, yogurt, cucumber, scallions, dill and some salt and pepper to taste. Serve immediately, or cover and leave until the salad cools to room temperature. Either way, stir in the toasted flaked almonds just before serving the salad.

CAESAR SALAD WITH FARFALLE Serves ❹

INGREDIENTS

14 ounces farfalle

salt

4 thick slices of a baguette

olive oil

3 Tbs mayonnaise

3 Tbs plain low-fat yogurt

½ romaine lettuce, shredded

4 scallions, trimmed and chopped

1⅓ cups Parmesan cheese, cut in flakes or coarsely grated

hot chili sauce, such as Tabasco, to taste

freshly ground black pepper

a little freshly chopped or torn parsley

This Caesar salad, with its creamy mayonnaise dressing and crunchy croutons, is made more substantial with the addition of pasta. It makes an excellent appetizer or light main course just as it is, or you could serve another salad, such as a simple tomato one, alongside it.

1 First fill a large saucepan with 4 quarts of water and bring to a boil over high heat for the pasta.

2 When the water boils, add the pasta along with a tablespoon of salt and give the pasta a quick stir. Briefly put the lid on until it starts to lift, showing that the water has come back to a boil, then let the pasta bubble away, uncovered, for about 8 minutes, or until it is tender but still has some bite to it.

3 Meanwhile, brush the slices of baguette with a little olive oil on each side and toast on both sides until crisp and golden. Cut into chunky croutons.

4 Drain the pasta by tipping it all into a colander placed in the sink, then put it back into the still-warm pan. Add the mayonnaise, yogurt, lettuce, scallions, half the Parmesan, the chili sauce and salt and pepper to taste, and stir gently until everything is combined.

5 Just before you want to serve the salad, stir in the croutons and scatter with the parsley and remaining Parmesan.

CONCHIGLIE IN CURRIED MAYONNAISE WITH RAISINS, CELERY, SCALLIONS AND CILANTRO Serves ❹

INGREDIENTS

⅓ cup raisins

14 ounces conchiglie

salt

3 Tbs mayonnaise

3 Tbs plain low-fat yogurt

curry paste to taste

freshly ground black pepper

1 celery heart, trimmed and sliced

4 scallions, trimmed and chopped

3–4 Tbs roughly chopped fresh cilantro

This is good served with some poppadums for a crisp contrast – or serve it with roasted cashew nuts or peanuts and perhaps mango chutney.

1 First fill a large saucepan with 4 quarts of water and bring to a boil over high heat for the pasta.

2 Meanwhile, put the raisins into a small bowl, cover with boiling water and leave to plump up.

3 When the pasta water boils, add the pasta along with a tablespoon of salt and give the pasta a quick stir. Briefly put the lid on until it starts to lift, showing that the water has come back to a boil, then let the pasta bubble away, uncovered, for about 8 minutes, or until it is tender but still has some bite to it.

4 Mix the mayonnaise with the yogurt and curry paste to your taste, and season with salt and pepper.

5 Drain the pasta by tipping it all into a colander placed in the sink, then put it back into the pan and add the mayonnaise mixture. Drain the raisins and add to the mixture, with the celery and scallions. Check the seasoning, then serve immediately, or cover and leave until the salad cools to room temperature. Scatter with a generous amount of fresh cilantro just before serving.

FUSILLI VINAIGRETTE WITH ZUCCHINI, AVOCADO AND SUMMER HERBS Serves ❹ as a main course, ❻ to ❽ as an appetizer

INGREDIENTS

14 ounces fusilli

salt

1 pound zucchini, trimmed and cut into ¼ inch slices (or matchsticks)

3 Tbs olive oil

1 Tbs wine vinegar

½ tsp Dijon mustard

1 garlic clove, peeled and crushed

freshly ground black pepper

1 avocado

1 Tbs freshly chopped or torn flat-leaf parsley

1 Tbs freshly chopped or torn chervil

1 Tbs freshly chopped chives

Gentle flavors and refreshing colors make this a favorite summer salad. It can be served as a main course, perhaps with some bread and an additional salad (made from plum tomatoes and fresh basil, for example), or served in smaller portions as an appetizer.

1 First fill a large saucepan with 4 quarts of water and bring to a boil over high heat for the pasta.

2 When the water boils, add the pasta along with a tablespoon of salt and give the pasta a quick stir. Briefly put the lid on until it starts to lift, showing that the water has come back to a boil, then let the pasta bubble away, uncovered, for about 8 minutes, or until it is tender but still has some bite to it.

3 Meanwhile, cook the zucchini in a little boiling water for 3–4 minutes until tender. Drain the zucchini.

4 Make a vinaigrette by putting the oil, vinegar, mustard, garlic and a seasoning of salt and pepper into a jar and shaking until combined.

5 Halve the avocado, spear the pit with the tip of a knife and pull it out, then peel off the skin. Slice the flesh.

6 Drain the pasta by tipping it all into a colander placed in the sink, then put it back into the still-warm pan. Add the cooked zucchini, the avocado and herbs. Give the vinaigrette a quick shake, then add to the pasta and stir gently until everything is coated. Serve immediately, before the avocado loses its bright color.

ORZO SALAD WITH LEMON, OLIVES AND FRESH HERBS Serves ❹

INGREDIENTS

14 ounces orzo

salt

3 Tbs olive oil

1 Tbs lemon juice

finely grated or thinly pared rind of ½ lemon

½ tsp Dijon mustard

1 garlic clove, peeled and crushed

freshly ground black pepper

⅓ cup black olives

8 sun-dried tomatoes, chopped

4 Tbs freshly chopped herbs

Orzo, a fine, small pasta not unlike rice or couscous, makes an excellent base for all kinds of delicious salads. Start with a good vinaigrette and then add salad ingredients to your taste.

1 First fill a large saucepan with 4 quarts of water and bring to a boil over high heat for the pasta.

2 When the water boils, add the pasta along with a tablespoon of salt and give the pasta a quick stir. Briefly put the lid on until it starts to lift, showing that the water has come back to a boil, then let the pasta bubble away, uncovered, for about 6 minutes, or until it is tender but still has some bite to it.

3 Make a vinaigrette by putting the oil, lemon juice and rind, mustard, garlic and a seasoning of salt and pepper into a jar and shaking until combined.

4 Drain the pasta by tipping it all into a colander placed in the sink, then put it back into the still-warm pan. Give the vinaigrette a quick shake, then add to the pasta, along with the olives, sun-dried tomatoes and herbs, and stir gently until everything is coated. Serve immediately, or cover and leave until the salad cools to room temperature.

FUSILLI AND CHICKPEA SALAD WITH SCALLIONS Serves ❹

INGREDIENTS

14 ounces fusilli

salt

3 Tbs olive oil

1 Tbs wine vinegar

1 garlic clove, peeled and crushed

freshly ground black pepper

14 ounces canned chickpeas, drained

bunch of scallions, trimmed and chopped

⅔ cup crème fraîche, optional

This simple salad is good served with an interesting bread, such as walnut or sun-dried tomato. The crème fraîche is optional, but delicious for a treat.

1 First fill a large saucepan with 4 quarts of water and bring to a boil over high heat for the pasta.

2 When the water boils, add the pasta along with a tablespoon of salt and give the pasta a quick stir. Briefly put the lid on until it starts to lift, showing that the water has come back to a boil, then let the pasta bubble away, uncovered, for about 8 minutes, or until it is tender but still has some bite to it.

3 Make a vinaigrette by putting the oil, vinegar, garlic and a seasoning of salt and pepper into a jar and shaking until combined.

4 Drain the pasta by tipping it all into a colander placed in the sink, then put it back into the still-warm pan. Add the chickpeas and scallions. Give the vinaigrette a quick shake, then add to the pasta and stir gently until everything is coated. Serve immediately, or cover and leave until the salad cools to room temperature. Either way, offer the crème fraîche separately, if using.

PASTA AND BEAN SALAD WITH CHILI-TOMATO VINAIGRETTE Serves ❹

INGREDIENTS

14 ounces any chunky pasta, such as farfalle, fusilli, conchiglie or penne

salt

3 Tbs olive oil

1 Tbs wine vinegar

1 Tbs sun-dried tomato paste

1 garlic clove, peeled and crushed

hot chili sauce, such as Tabasco, to taste

freshly ground black pepper

15 ounces canned red kidney beans, drained

1 mild onion, peeled and sliced

1 green bell pepper, de-seeded and finely chopped

2 Tbs freshly chopped cilantro or parsley

Pasta and any type of beans make a great combination, and served with some fresh leafy salad make a filling and satisfactory main course. You can add almost anything to the bean salad – trust your inspiration and the contents of your kitchen cupboard and fridge. You could use other types of canned beans, such as cannellini beans, black-eyed peas, flageolets or green lentils instead of the red kidney beans. Some grated carrot and/or sliced avocado is also good in this salad.

1 First fill a large saucepan with 4 quarts of water and bring to a boil over high heat for the pasta.

2 When the water boils, add the pasta along with a tablespoon of salt and give the pasta a quick stir. Briefly put the lid on until it starts to lift, showing that the water has come back to a boil, then let the pasta bubble away, uncovered, for about 8 minutes, or until it is tender but still has some bite to it.

3 Make a vinaigrette by putting the oil, vinegar, sun-dried tomato paste, garlic, chili sauce to your taste and a seasoning of salt and pepper into a jar and shaking until combined.

4 Drain the pasta by tipping it all into a colander placed in the sink, then put it back into the still-warm pan. Add the beans, onion and green pepper. Give the vinaigrette a quick shake, then add to the pasta, along with the chopped herbs, and stir gently until everything is coated. Serve immediately, or cover and leave until the salad cools to room temperature.

Five-Minute Sauces

This section is in the book at the request of my daughter Meg, a busy doctor who has little time for cooking during the week. As the name suggests, all the sauces or additions to the pasta can be prepared in five minutes, while the pasta cooks. Each dish can stand alone as a complete main course, although I like to serve them with a green or mixed salad on the side, and bread for those who want it.

Some of the dishes only need kitchen cupboard ingredients, and so are ideal for those times when you need to make a meal quickly and have had no time to shop. If you keep a few standby ingredients in the cupboard, along with pasta and olive oil, you will never be stuck for a quick meal. Good basics to keep on hand are: sun-dried tomatoes and sun-dried tomato paste, dried red chilies, dried porcini mushrooms, good-quality olive oil (of course), garlic and black olives. I do not use cans much besides these two: plum tomatoes and artichoke hearts, both of which are useful and good to have on hand. In the freezer it is useful to keep a package of frozen peas (I like petit pois) and one of corn kernels. Some pine nuts and any other type of nut that you like, such as walnuts and pecans, are useful to have, and best kept in the refrigerator or freezer if you have room. If you like Parmesan cheese, keep a piece of that in the refrigerator, too.

PENNE WITH VODKA AND PEAS Serves ❹

INGREDIENTS

14 ounces penne

salt

1½ cups shelled fresh peas or frozen petits pois

1 Tbs olive oil

½ cup vodka

freshly ground black pepper

With vodka added at the last minute, this dish definitely has an alcoholic kick to it. If you prefer, you can boil off the alcohol: simply allow the vodka to come briefly to a boil in the pasta pan.

1 First fill a large saucepan with 4 quarts of water and bring to a boil over high heat for the pasta.

2 When the water boils, add the pasta along with a tablespoon of salt and give the pasta a quick stir. Briefly put the lid on until it starts to lift, showing that the water has come back to a boil, then let the pasta bubble away, uncovered, for about 8 minutes, or until it is tender but still has some bite to it.

3 Just before the pasta is done, add the peas to it and cook briefly, just to heat the peas through.

4 Drain the pasta and peas by tipping them into a colander placed in the sink, then put them back into the still-warm pan, add the olive oil, vodka and a grinding of black pepper and serve on warm plates.

FARFALLE WITH SHIITAKE MUSHROOMS, PARMESAN AND SAGE Serves ❹

INGREDIENTS

14 ounces farfalle

salt

1 pound fresh shiitake mushrooms, cleaned and sliced

2 Tbs olive oil

1 garlic clove, peeled and crushed

6 fresh sage leaves, chopped

freshly ground black pepper

⅔ cup fresh Parmesan cheese shavings

Fresh shiitake mushrooms are good in this; otherwise try chestnut mushrooms.

1 First fill a large saucepan with 4 quarts of water and bring to a boil over high heat for the pasta.

2 When the water boils, add the pasta along with a tablespoon of salt and give the pasta a quick stir. Briefly put the lid on until it starts to lift, showing that the water has come back to a boil, then let the pasta bubble away, uncovered, for about 8 minutes, or until it is tender but still has some bite to it.

3 Meanwhile, fry the mushrooms in the olive oil, with the garlic, for 4–5 minutes, until tender and any liquid has boiled away. Stir in the sage and season with salt and pepper.

4 Drain the pasta by tipping it all into a colander placed in the sink, then put it back into the still-warm pan, add the mushroom and sage mixture and Parmesan, and serve on warm plates.

PENNE WITH SPINACH, MASCARPONE AND PARMESAN Serves ❹

INGREDIENTS

14 ounces penne

salt

½ cup mascarpone cheese, or reduced-fat cream cheese

1 pound baby spinach leaves, washed and shredded

freshly ground black pepper

fresh Parmesan cheese, cut in flakes or grated, to serve

A lovely, simple pasta dish that makes the most of the flavor of tender spinach leaves. As with the other mascarpone recipes in this book, you can substitute a reduced-fat cream cheese to save some calories if you wish.

1 First fill a large saucepan with 4 quarts of water and bring to a boil over high heat for the pasta.

2 When the water boils, add the pasta along with a tablespoon of salt and give the pasta a quick stir. Briefly put the lid on until it starts to lift, showing that the water has come back to a boil, then let the pasta bubble away, uncovered, for about 8 minutes, or until it is tender but still has some bite to it.

3 Drain the pasta by tipping it all into a colander placed in the sink, then put it back into the still-warm pan with the mascarpone cheese and stir gently until the cheese has heated through but not boiled. Add the shredded spinach, which will cook in the heat of the pasta, mix gently, season with salt and pepper and serve immediately on warm plates with the Parmesan on top.

FARFALLE WITH SNOW PEAS, LEMON AND BASIL Serves ❹

INGREDIENTS

14 ounces farfalle

salt

12 ounces snow peas, trimmed

2 Tbs olive oil

finely grated or thinly pared rind of 1 lemon

juice of 1 lemon

freshly ground black pepper

4 good sprigs of fresh basil leaves

Nice and simple and fresh-tasting, this is good served either as an appetizer or as a light summer dish.

1 First fill a large saucepan with 4 quarts of water and bring to a boil over high heat for the pasta.

2 When the water boils, add the pasta along with a tablespoon of salt and give the pasta a quick stir. Briefly put the lid on until it starts to lift, showing that the water has come back to a boil, then let the pasta bubble away, uncovered, for about 8 minutes, or until it is tender but still has some bite to it.

3 Just before the pasta is done, add the snow peas to it and cook briefly, just to heat through.

4 Drain the pasta and snow peas by tipping them into a colander placed in the sink, then put them back into the still-warm pan, add the olive oil, lemon rind and juice and a grinding of black pepper, and serve on warm plates. Tear the basil over the top.

LASAGNETTE WITH SUN-DRIED TOMATOES, GARLIC AND BASIL Serves ❹

INGREDIENTS

INGREDIENTS

14 ounces lasagnette

salt

2 garlic cloves, peeled and crushed

1 Tbs olive oil

4 Tbs sun-dried tomato paste or chopped sun-dried tomatoes

freshly ground black pepper

fresh basil leaves and flakes of Parmesan cheese, to serve

Ultra quick and very good, this recipe makes the most of the intense rich flavor of sun-dried tomatoes.

1 First fill a large saucepan with 4 quarts of water and bring to a boil over high heat for the pasta.

2 When the water boils, add the pasta along with a tablespoon of salt and give the pasta a quick stir. Briefly put the lid on until it starts to lift, showing that the water has come back to a boil. Then let the pasta bubble away, uncovered, for about 8 minutes, or until it is tender but still has some bite to it.

3 Just before the pasta is done, cook the garlic in the olive oil over low heat for 2–3 minutes, without letting it brown.

4 Drain the pasta by tipping it all into a colander placed in the sink, then put it back into the still-warm pan, pour in the garlic and its oil and add the sun-dried tomato paste or chopped sun-dried tomatoes and some pepper. Stir gently, then serve on warm plates. Tear the basil over and scatter the Parmesan on top.

SPAGHETTI WITH GARLIC AND OLIVE OIL Serves ❹

INGREDIENTS

14 ounces spaghetti

salt

2–4 fat juicy garlic cloves, peeled and sliced, chopped or crushed

2–4 Tbs olive oil

freshly ground black pepper

freshly grated Parmesan cheese, to serve, optional

This is the simplest pasta dish in the world. The better the ingredients, the better this dish will be. The garlic can be chopped, crushed or sliced – I prefer it sliced. The amount of oil you add to this recipe is up to you; I do not like it too oily, but you need enough in this recipe to give flavor and moistness to the dish.

1 First fill a large saucepan with 4 quarts of water and bring to a boil over high heat for the pasta.

2 When the water boils, add the spaghetti, holding it straight up like a bunch of flowers and gently pushing it into the water as it softens. Add a tablespoon of salt and give the pasta a quick stir. Briefly put the lid on until it starts to lift, showing that the water has come back to a boil. Then let the pasta bubble away, uncovered, for about 8 minutes, or until it is tender but still has some bite to it.

3 Meanwhile, cook the garlic in the olive oil over low heat – it needs just to soften and warm through without browning.

4 Drain the pasta by tipping it all into a colander placed in the sink, then put it back into the still-warm pan, add the garlic and its oil along with a good grinding of salt and pepper as needed, toss gently and serve on warm plates. Hand around the Parmesan, if desired.

SPAGHETTI WITH OLIVE OIL AND RED CHILI FLAKES Serves ❹

INGREDIENTS

14 ounces spaghetti

salt

2 garlic cloves, peeled and finely chopped

2–4 Tbs olive oil

1–2 dried red chilies, crumbled

freshly ground black pepper

fresh Parmesan cheese, cut in flakes or grated, to serve, optional

torn or chopped fresh flat-leaf parsley, to serve, optional

So simple to make, yet so good, in this recipe the amounts of chili, garlic and olive oil can be varied to suit your taste. Little dried red chilies (which you can buy at any supermarket) are very hot, so go carefully.

1 First fill a large saucepan with 4 quarts of water and bring to a boil over high heat for the pasta.

2 When the water in the saucepan boils, add the spaghetti, holding it straight up like a bunch of flowers and gently pushing it into the water as it softens. Add a tablespoon of salt and give the pasta a quick stir. Briefly put the lid on until it starts to lift, showing that the water has come back to a boil, then let the pasta bubble away, uncovered, for about 8 minutes, or until it is tender but still has some bite to it.

3 Just before the pasta is done, cook the garlic in the olive oil over low heat for 2–3 minutes without letting it brown. Then add the chili – stand back, as the oil released by chili on contact with heat can make you cough – and stir-fry for a few seconds. Leave on one side until the spaghetti is done.

4 Drain the pasta by tipping it all into a colander placed in the sink, then put it back into the still-warm pan. Quickly reheat the garlic mixture, then pour it onto the pasta. Stir gently, season with salt and pepper as necessary, then serve it on warm plates and top with some Parmesan and/or parsley, according to your taste.

FUSILLI WITH GARLIC AND HERB CREAM CHEESE AND YOUNG PEAS Serves ❹

INGREDIENTS

14 ounces fusilli

salt

1½ cups shelled fresh young peas or frozen petits pois

⅔ cup garlic and herb cream cheese, full fat or reduced fat

Fresh peas are delicious in this if you can get them; otherwise, frozen petits pois make a good substitute.

1 First fill a large saucepan with 4 quarts of water and bring to a boil over high heat for the pasta.

2 When the water in the saucepan boils, add the pasta along with a tablespoon of salt and give the pasta a quick stir. Briefly put the lid on until it starts to lift, showing that the water has come back to a boil, then let the

pasta bubble away, uncovered, for about 8 minutes, or until it is tender but still has some bite to it.

3 Just before the pasta is done, add the peas to it and cook briefly, just to heat the peas through.

4 Drain the pasta and peas by tipping them into a colander placed in the sink, then put them back into the still-warm pan with the cream cheese, toss gently and serve on warm plates.

GNOCCHI WITH MUSHROOMS, ARTICHOKES, MASCARPONE AND FRESH BASIL Serves ❹

INGREDIENTS

14 ounces gnocchi

salt

12 ounces mushrooms, cleaned and sliced

1 Tbs olive oil

1 garlic clove, peeled and crushed

14 ounces canned artichoke hearts, drained and sliced

½ cup mascarpone cheese, or reduced-fat cream cheese

freshly ground black pepper

fresh basil leaves, to serve

Serve this creamy pasta dish with some crisp garlic bread. Mascarpone is luscious but high in calories; for a less rich dish, use a reduced-fat cream cheese instead.

1 First fill a large saucepan with 4 quarts of water and bring to a boil over high heat for the pasta.

2 When the water boils, add the pasta along with a tablespoon of salt and give the pasta a quick stir. Briefly put the lid on until it starts to lift, showing that the water has come back to a boil, then let the pasta bubble away, uncovered, for about 8 minutes, or until it is tender but still has some bite to it.

3 Sauté the mushrooms in the olive oil, with the garlic, for 4–5 minutes, until tender and any liquid has boiled away. Add the artichoke hearts and continue to cook gently until they are heated through.

4 Drain the pasta by tipping it all into a colander placed in the sink, then put it back into the still-warm pan with the mascarpone cheese and stir gently until the cheese has heated through but not boiled. Add the mushroom and artichoke mixture, mix gently and season with salt and pepper. Serve immediately on warm plates with a generous amount of fresh basil torn or snipped over the top.

FARFALLE WITH MUSHROOMS, PEAS AND PARSLEY Serves ❹

INGREDIENTS

14 ounces farfalle

salt

12 ounces mushrooms, cleaned and sliced

2 Tbs butter

1 Tbs olive oil

1 garlic clove, peeled and crushed

1½ cups shelled fresh peas, frozen petits pois or trimmed snow peas

2 Tbs chopped fresh parsley, flat-leaf if available, to serve

Regular domestic mushrooms are fine for this, as are frozen petits pois, although if you can get fresh peas or snow peas they would be even better.

1 First fill a large saucepan with 4 quarts of water and bring to a boil over high heat for the pasta.

2 When the water boils, add the pasta along with a tablespoon of salt and give the pasta a quick stir. Briefly put the lid on until it starts to lift, showing that the water has come back to a boil, then let the pasta bubble away, uncovered, for about 8 minutes, or until it is tender but still has some bite to it.

3 Sauté the mushrooms in the butter and olive oil, with the garlic, for 4–5 minutes, until tender and any liquid has boiled away.

4 Just before the pasta is done, add the peas (or snow peas) to it and cook briefly, just to heat them through.

5 Drain the pasta and peas by tipping them into a colander placed in the sink, then put them back into the still-warm pan, add the mushrooms, toss gently and serve on warm plates with the parsley on top.

TAGLIATELLE, STILTON AND PECANS Serves ❹

INGREDIENTS

14 ounces tagliatelle, plain
or verde

salt

½ cup light cream or pasta
cooking water

1 garlic clove, peeled and crushed

6 ounces Stilton cheese

freshly ground black pepper

½ cup pecans, coarsely
chopped, toasted (see page 78)

This recipe was invented by my daughter Meg. Other blue cheeses can be substituted for the Stilton, and a mixed salad makes a good accompaniment. For a lower-fat version, you can use some of the pasta cooking water instead of the light cream for melting the cheese.

1 First fill a large saucepan with 4 quarts of water and bring to a boil over high heat for the pasta.

2 When the water boils, add the pasta along with a tablespoon of salt and give the pasta a quick stir. Briefly put the lid on until it starts to lift, showing that the water has come back to a boil, then let the pasta bubble away, uncovered, for about 8 minutes, or until it is tender but still has some bite to it.

3 Just before the pasta is ready, heat the cream (or the same quantity of water, scooped from the pasta pan) in a small saucepan, add the garlic and crumble in the Stilton cheese. Stir over low heat until the cheese has melted and combined with the liquid to make a creamy sauce – do not let it overheat.

4 Drain the pasta by tipping it all into a colander placed in the sink, then put it back into the still-warm pan and add the cheese mixture. Grind black pepper over, toss gently and serve on warm plates, scattered with the pecans.

MACARONI, CHEDDAR CHEESE AND CHERRY TOMATOES Serves ❹

INGREDIENTS

14 ounces macaroni

salt

1 Tbs olive oil

12 ounces cherry tomatoes, halved

1½ cups coarsely grated Cheddar
cheese, or cut into small dice

Simple, fresh and pretty to look at, this dish appeals particularly to children.

1 First fill a large saucepan with 4 quarts of water and bring to a boil over high heat for the pasta.

2 When the water boils, add the pasta along with a tablespoon of salt and give the pasta a quick stir. Briefly put the lid on until it starts to lift, showing that the water has come back to a boil, then let the pasta bubble away, uncovered, for about 8 minutes, or until it is tender but still has some bite to it.

3 Drain the pasta by tipping it all into a colander placed in the sink, then put it back into the still-warm pan, add the olive oil and toss gently before adding the tomatoes and cheese. Mix again, to combine, then serve on warm plates.

FETTUCCINE WITH PEAS, GRUYÈRE AND CREAM Serves ❹

INGREDIENTS

14 ounces fettuccine

salt

⅓ cup light cream

1 cup grated Gruyère cheese

1½ cups shelled fresh peas or frozen petits pois

In this recipe, the cheese is melted in the cream to make a sauce that is then mixed with the pasta and peas. It is rich, so serve it with a simple tomato or leafy salad to provide the perfect balance.

1 First fill a large saucepan with 4 quarts of water and bring to a boil over high heat for the pasta.

2 When the water boils, add the pasta along with a tablespoon of salt and give the pasta a quick stir. Briefly put the lid on until it starts to lift, showing that the water has come back to a boil, then let the pasta bubble away, uncovered, for about 8 minutes, or until it is tender but still has some bite to it.

3 Meanwhile, heat the cream and cheese in a small saucepan over low heat until the cheese has melted, then remove from the heat.

4 Just before the pasta is done, add the peas to it and cook briefly, just to heat the peas through. Quickly reheat the cheese mixture, but do not let it boil.

5 Drain the pasta and peas by tipping them into a colander placed in the sink, then put them back into the still-warm pan, add the cheese mixture, toss gently and serve on warm plates.

FETTUCCINE WITH SUN-DRIED TOMATOES, GARLIC AND BASIL Serves ❹

INGREDIENTS

14 ounces fettuccine

salt

2–4 fat juicy garlic cloves, peeled and sliced

2–4 Tbs olive oil or oil from the sun-dried tomatoes

12 sun-dried tomatoes, chopped

freshly ground black pepper

fresh basil leaves and flakes of Parmesan cheese, to serve

I love the intense flavor of sun-dried tomatoes. For texture and appearance in this recipe I use whole ones, which I slice, but you could equally well use sun-dried tomato paste if you prefer.

1 First fill a large saucepan with 4 quarts of water and bring to a boil over high heat for the pasta.

2 When the water boils, add the pasta along with a tablespoon of salt and give the pasta a quick stir. Briefly put the lid on until it starts to lift, showing that the water has come back to a boil, then let the pasta bubble away, uncovered, for about 8 minutes, or until it is tender but still has some bite to it.

3 Meanwhile, sauté the garlic in the olive or sun-dried-tomato oil over low heat – it needs just to soften and warm through without browning. Just before the pasta is done, add the sun-dried tomatoes to the garlic mixture and warm them through over the heat, too.

4 Drain the pasta by tipping it all into a colander placed in the sink, then put it back into the still-warm pan, add the garlic mixture and salt and pepper to taste, toss gently and serve on warm plates. Tear the basil over and scatter the Parmesan on top.

PENNONI WITH AVOCADO, CHILI AND CILANTRO Serves ❹

INGREDIENTS

14 ounces pennoni

salt

1 garlic clove, peeled and crushed

1 fresh green chili, de-seeded and finely sliced

1 Tbs olive oil

1 avocado, peeled and sliced

juice of 1 lemon

freshly ground black pepper

4 Tbs roughly chopped fresh cilantro, to serve

We do not often think of avocado in terms of a hot pasta dish, but this is a combination I like. It is important not to let the avocado get too hot or the flavor will be spoiled. Some crunchy garlic bread goes well with this dish, and maybe a tomato salad too.

1 First fill a large saucepan with 4 quarts of water and bring to a boil over high heat for the pasta.

2 When the water boils, add the pasta along with a tablespoon of salt and give the pasta a quick stir. Briefly put the lid on until it starts to lift, showing that the water has come back to a boil, then let the pasta bubble away, uncovered, for about 8 minutes, or until it is tender but still has some bite to it.

3 Meanwhile, sauté the garlic and chili in the olive oil over low heat for 2–3 minutes, until softened but not browned. Keep on one side.

4 Toss the avocado in the lemon juice and season with salt and pepper.

5 Drain the pasta by tipping it all into a colander placed in the sink, then put it back into the still-warm pan and add the chili mixture and avocado. Toss gently and serve on warm plates, with the cilantro on top.

TAGLIATELLE WITH GREEN PEPPERCORNS Serves ❹

INGREDIENTS

14 ounces tagliatelle

salt

2–4 Tbs olive oil

1 Tbs green peppercorns

freshly ground black pepper

freshly chopped parsley or chervil, to serve

freshly grated Parmesan or pecorino cheese, to serve

Piquant green peppercorns make a pleasant contrast with bland pasta. This is also good made with spaghetti or one of the short pastas, such as penne, if you prefer.

1 First fill a large saucepan with 4 quarts of water and bring to a boil over high heat for the pasta.

2 When the water boils, add the pasta along with a tablespoon of salt and give the pasta a quick stir. Briefly put the lid on until it starts to lift, showing that the water has come back to a boil, then let the pasta bubble away, uncovered, for about 8 minutes, or until it is tender but still has some bite to it.

3 Drain the pasta by tipping it all into a colander placed in the sink, then put it back into the still-warm pan, add the olive oil, green peppercorns and salt and black pepper to taste, toss gently and serve on warm plates, with herbs and cheese scattered over the top.

FETTUCCINE WITH LEMON Serves ❹

INGREDIENTS

14 ounces fettuccine

salt

1 fat juicy garlic clove, peeled
and crushed

2–4 Tbs olive oil

finely grated or thinly pared rind of
1 lemon

juice of 1 lemon

freshly ground black pepper

freshly torn flat-leaf parsley, to
serve, optional

freshly grated Parmesan cheese, to
serve, optional

This is a delicate combination of flavors. If you have a zester and can make thin strands of lemon rind, they look particularly pretty with the fettuccine.

1 First fill a large saucepan with 4 quarts of water and bring to a boil over high heat for the pasta.

2 When the water boils, add the pasta along with a tablespoon of salt and give the pasta a quick stir. Briefly put the lid on until it starts to lift, showing that the water has come back to a boil, then let the pasta bubble away, uncovered, for about 8 minutes, or until it is tender but still has some bite to it.

3 Meanwhile, sauté the garlic in the olive oil over low heat for 2–3 minutes, without letting it brown. Keep on one side.

4 Drain the pasta by tipping it all into a colander placed in the sink, then put it back into the still-warm pan. Add the garlic and its oil, the lemon rind and juice and plenty of black pepper. Toss gently, then serve on warm plates with parsley and Parmesan on the top, if using.

TAGLIATELLE WITH WALNUTS AND WALNUT OIL Serves ❹

INGREDIENTS

14 ounces tagliatelle

salt

1 garlic clove, peeled and crushed

1 Tbs olive oil

2 Tbs walnut oil

1½–2 cups shelled walnuts
(preferably freshly cracked),
coarsely chopped

freshly ground black pepper

freshly chopped parsley, to
serve, optional

fresh Parmesan cheese, cut in flakes
or grated, to serve, optional

This is nicest when made with freshly cracked walnuts – it is well worth the trouble if time and patience permit.

1 First fill a large saucepan with 4 quarts of water and bring to a boil over high heat for the pasta.

2 When the water boils, add the pasta along with a tablespoon of salt and give the pasta a quick stir. Briefly put the lid on until it starts to lift, showing that the water has come back to a boil, then let the pasta bubble away, uncovered, for about 8 minutes, or until it is tender but still has some bite to it.

3 Meanwhile, sauté the garlic in the olive oil over low heat for 2–3 minutes, without letting it brown. Keep on one side.

4 Drain the pasta by tipping it all into a colander placed in the sink, then put it back into the still-warm pan. Add the olive oil and garlic mixture, the walnut oil and walnuts, and grind over black pepper to taste. Toss gently, then serve on warm plates, with parsley and Parmesan on top, if using.

FETTUCCINE WITH RADICCHIO AND PINK PEPPERCORNS Serves ❹

INGREDIENTS

14 ounces fettuccine

salt

olive oil

1 radicchio, finely shredded

freshly ground black pepper

1 Tbs pink peppercorns, lightly crushed

A salad of mixed leaves, including some radicchio and mâche lettuce, with a light dressing, goes well with this.

1 First fill a large saucepan with 4 quarts of water and bring to a boil over high heat for the pasta.

2 When the water boils, add the pasta along with a tablespoon of salt and give the pasta a quick stir. Briefly put the lid on until it starts to lift, showing that the water has come back to a boil, then let the pasta bubble away, uncovered, for about 8 minutes, or until it is tender but still has some bite to it.

3 Just before the pasta is done, heat 2 tablespoons olive oil in a saucepan and stir-fry the radicchio in it for 1–2 minutes, until wilted.

4 Drain the pasta by tipping it all into a colander placed in the sink, then put it back into the still-warm pan. Quickly reheat the radicchio, then tip it into the pasta, including the oil, and stir the pasta gently. Add a little extra olive oil if desired, then season with black pepper. Serve the pasta on warm plates and scatter the crushed pink peppercorns on top.

FUSILLI LUNGHI WITH SPINACH, PINE NUTS AND RAISINS Serves ❹

INGREDIENTS

14 ounces fusilli lunghi

salt

2 Tbs olive oil

1 pound tender spinach leaves, washed

⅓ cup raisins

freshly ground black pepper

½ cup pine nuts, toasted (see page 78)

Spinach, pine nuts and raisins is a classic combination in Catalan cuisine, and one that I love.

1 First fill a large saucepan with 4 quarts of water and bring to a boil over high heat for the pasta.

2 When the water boils, add the pasta along with a tablespoon of salt and give the pasta a quick stir. Briefly put the lid on until it starts to lift, showing that the water has come back to a boil, then let the pasta bubble away, uncovered, for about 8 minutes, or until it is tender but still has some bite to it.

3 Meanwhile, heat the olive oil in a large pan and put in the spinach. Stir-fry over high heat for 2–3 minutes until wilted, then add the raisins and season with salt and pepper.

4 Drain the pasta by tipping it all into a colander placed in the sink, then put it back into the still-warm pan, add the spinach mixture and the pine nuts and toss gently. Serve on warm plates.

FETTUCCINE IN THE SOUTHERN ITALIAN STYLE WITH ARUGULA AND DILL Serves ❹

INGREDIENTS

14 ounces fettuccine

salt

2–4 fat juicy garlic cloves, peeled and chopped or thinly sliced

4 Tbs olive oil

8 ounces arugula, chopped

4 good sprigs of dill, chopped

freshly ground black pepper

freshly chopped parsley or chervil, to serve

freshly grated or flaked pecorino cheese, to serve, optional

You really need a substantial bunch of arugula to make this – those little supermarket packages do not contain enough and cost too much to make it worthwhile. The best place to find bunches of arugula is often a Middle Eastern store.

1 First fill a large saucepan with 4 quarts of water and bring to a boil over high heat for the pasta.

2 When the water boils, add the pasta along with a tablespoon of salt and give the pasta a quick stir. Briefly put the lid on until it starts to lift, showing that the water has come back to a boil, then let the pasta bubble away, uncovered, for about 8 minutes, or until it is tender but still has some bite to it.

3 Meanwhile, sauté the garlic in the olive oil over low heat for 2–3 minutes, without letting it brown. Keep on one side.

4 Drain the pasta by tipping it all into a colander placed in the sink, then put it back into the still-warm pan. Add the garlic and oil, then throw in the arugula and dill, toss gently over the heat so that they warm through briefly, and grind in black pepper to taste. Serve on warm plates, scatter with parsley and chervil and hand around the pecorino cheese, if using.

LUMACHE WITH WILD MUSHROOMS Serves ❹

INGREDIENTS

14 ounces lumache

salt

1–1½ pounds wild mushrooms, cleaned and sliced as necessary

2 Tbs olive oil

2 garlic cloves, peeled and crushed

squeeze of lemon juice

freshly ground black pepper

roughly chopped fresh parsley, preferably flat-leaf, to serve, optional

fresh Parmesan cheese, cut in flakes or grated, to serve, optional

You can use any mixture of wild mushrooms for this – or even regular domestic ones with just a few more interesting ones added. It is a wonderful combination – the more mushrooms the better.

1 First fill a large saucepan with 4 quarts of water and bring to a boil over high heat for the pasta.

2 When the water boils, add the pasta along with a tablespoon of salt and give the pasta a quick stir. Briefly put the lid on until it starts to lift, showing that the water has come back to a boil, then let the pasta bubble away, uncovered, for about 8 minutes, or until it is tender but still has some bite to it.

3 Meanwhile, sauté the mushrooms in the olive oil, with the garlic, for 4–5 minutes, until tender and any liquid has boiled away. Add a squeeze of lemon juice to bring out the flavor, then season with salt and pepper.

4 Drain the pasta by tipping it all into a colander placed in the sink, then put it back into the still-warm pan, add the mushrooms, toss gently and check the seasoning, adding more salt and pepper if necessary. Serve on warm plates, and scatter the parsley and Parmesan over the top, if using.

PENNE WITH ARUGULA, PINE NUTS AND PARMESAN Serves ❹

INGREDIENTS

14 ounces penne

salt

6 cups arugula

2 garlic cloves, peeled and finely sliced or chopped

olive oil

freshly ground black pepper

squeeze of lemon juice

½ cup pine nuts, toasted (see page 78)

⅔ cup freshly grated or flaked Parmesan cheese

If you can buy arugula by the bunch it will be much cheaper and you will be able to use it with abandon. It is also very easy to grow, though it can go to seed so you need to keep sowing it throughout the summer.

1 First fill a large saucepan with 4 quarts of water and bring to a boil over high heat for the pasta.

2 When the water boils, add the pasta along with a tablespoon of salt and give the pasta a quick stir. Briefly put the lid on until it starts to lift, showing that the water has come back to a boil, then let the pasta bubble away, uncovered, for about 8 minutes, or until it is tender but still has some bite to it.

3 Just before the pasta is done, stir-fry the arugula with the garlic in 2 tablespoons of olive oil for 2–3 minutes, until the arugula is wilted. Season with salt, pepper and a squeeze of lemon juice.

4 Drain the pasta by tipping it all into a colander placed in the sink, then put it back into the still-warm pan. Quickly reheat the arugula, then add it to the pasta, along with a little extra olive oil if you think the mixture needs it, and the pine nuts and Parmesan. Toss gently, check the seasoning, then serve on warm plates.

FETTUCCINE WITH BUTTER AND DOLCELATTE Serves ❹

INGREDIENTS

14 ounces fettuccine

salt

4 Tbs butter

6 ounces dolcelatte cheese

freshly ground black pepper

The sauce is rich but full of flavor, so a little goes a long way. If you cannot get dolcelatte cheese, use Gorgonzola or another blue cheese, such as Danish blue. A leafy salad, including some hot leaves, such as arugula or watercress, goes well with this.

1 First fill a large saucepan with 4 quarts of water and bring to a boil over high heat for the pasta.

2 When the water boils, add the pasta along with a tablespoon of salt and give the pasta a quick stir. Briefly put the lid on until it starts to lift, showing that the water has come back to a boil, then let the pasta bubble away, uncovered, for about 8 minutes, or until it is tender but still has some bite to it.

3 Just before the pasta is ready, melt the butter in a small saucepan, crumble in the cheese and stir over low heat until it has melted and combined with the butter to make a creamy sauce – do not let it overheat.

4 Drain the pasta by tipping it all into a colander placed in the sink, then put it back into the still-warm pan and add the cheese mixture. Grind black pepper over, toss gently and serve on warm plates.

Simple Pasta Dishes

*T*hese take a little longer to make than the Five-Minute Sauces but they are still pretty quick and some of them, such as Lumache with feta cheese and broccoli, and Pipe rigate with Swiss chard, mascarpone and pine nuts, take less than ten minutes.

Other recipes which take longer can often be partly prepared in advance then quickly assembled at the last minute. For instance, if you want to make Penne with roasted Mediterranean vegetables, you could roast the vegetables earlier in the day, or even the day before, and keep them covered and cool, ready for later. Even Pennoni with croutons and caramelized onions could be partially prepared in advance: although the onions take half an hour to cook, they will not spoil if you leave them for a few hours then reheat them just before you serve the pasta.

As with all the recipes in this book, I have specified the type of pasta that I think goes best with the ingredients in the recipe. If you do not agree, or do not have that particular pasta available, by all means make changes and substitutions. Enjoy the recipes and make them your own.

Soy sauce is used in one or two of the recipes in this section, and in other recipes in the book. It is worth seeking out a good soy sauce, properly fermented and made just from soy beans and water without additions, such as caramel. Look for Chinese or Japanese brands; a health food store will have them, as will a large supermarket.

ORECCHIETTE WITH OYSTER MUSHROOMS, LEEKS AND SUN-DRIED TOMATOES Serves ❹

INGREDIENTS

8 ounces leeks, trimmed and cut into ¼ inch slices

2 Tbs olive oil, or oil from the sun-dried tomatoes (see below)

14 ounces orecchiette

salt

8 ounces oyster mushrooms, washed and sliced

8 sun-dried tomatoes, chopped

freshly ground black pepper

fresh basil leaves and flakes of Parmesan cheese, to serve

This is a lovely, rich-tasting mixture; I like to serve it with a simple green salad.

1 First fill a large saucepan with 4 quarts of water and bring to a boil over high heat for the pasta.

2 Meanwhile, cook the leeks, either by sautéing in 1 tablespoon of oil or, for a less rich result, in a little boiling water. Either way they will take about 6 minutes. Drain the leeks if necessary and keep them warm.

3 When the water in the saucepan boils, add the pasta along with a tablespoon of salt and give the pasta a quick stir. Briefly put the lid on until it starts to lift, showing that the water has come back to a boil, then let the pasta bubble away, uncovered, for about 8 minutes, or until it is tender but still has some bite to it.

4 Meanwhile, heat the remaining oil in a saucepan and fry the mushrooms for 4–5 minutes until tender.

5 Drain the pasta by tipping it all into a colander placed in the sink, then put it back into the still-warm pan. Add the leeks, the mushrooms with their oil, sun-dried tomatoes and a seasoning of salt and pepper to taste. Serve the pasta on warm plates, tear the basil leaves over the pasta and scatter the Parmesan on top.

PENNE WITH ROASTED MEDITERRANEAN VEGETABLES Serves ❹

INGREDIENTS

1 eggplant, cut into ½ inch dice

2 Tbs olive oil

2 red bell peppers, de-seeded and cut into ½ inch squares

2 yellow bell peppers, de-seeded and cut into ½ inch squares

4 tomatoes, halved

4 large garlic cloves, peeled and chopped

salt and freshly ground black pepper

14 ounces penne

fresh basil leaves and flakes of Parmesan cheese, to serve

The vegetables for this recipe can be roasted ahead of time – even the day before, if convenient, when the oven is on for something else. Then you can put the dish together very quickly, simply reheating the vegetables in the oven, broiler or microwave before adding them to the cooked pasta.

1 Toss the eggplant in the olive oil, using your fingers to make sure that each piece is coated. Put the eggplant pieces into a shallow roasting pan with the peppers and roast in a medium-hot oven for 20 minutes. Then add the tomatoes and garlic and roast for a further 15–30 minutes, until all the vegetables are tender and lightly browned. Season with salt and pepper to taste.

2 Fill a large saucepan with 4 quarts of water and bring to a boil for the pasta.

3 When the water boils, add the pasta along with a tablespoon of salt and give the pasta a quick stir. Briefly put the lid on until it starts to lift, showing that the water has come back to a boil, then let the pasta bubble away, uncovered, for about 8 minutes, or until it is tender but still has some bite to it.

4 Drain the pasta by tipping it all into a colander placed in the sink, then put it back into the still-warm pan and add the vegetables. Toss gently and serve on warm plates. Tear the basil over and scatter the Parmesan on top.

SPAGHETTINI WITH TOFU, SOY SAUCE AND PEANUTS Serves ❹

INGREDIENTS

4 Tbs soy sauce, such
as Kikkoman

2 garlic cloves, peeled and crushed

1 tsp grated fresh ginger

1 dried red chili, crumbled

10 ounces firm tofu, drained

14 ounces spaghettini

salt

peanut oil

1 Tbs sesame oil

4 scallions, trimmed and chopped

½–1 cup roasted peanuts, crushed

freshly ground black pepper

freshly chopped cilantro leaves,
to serve

This dish has an Eastern flavor and a pleasant contrast of textures.

1 First prepare the tofu: this is best done at least half an hour before you start cooking the pasta, and can be done several hours in advance. Mix the soy sauce with the garlic, ginger and chili. Cut the tofu into thin slices, spread these out in a single layer on a plate, then spoon the soy sauce mixture over, making sure all the tofu gets coated. Leave to marinate.

2 Fill a large saucepan with 4 quarts of water and bring to a boil over high heat for the pasta.

3 When the water boils, add the spaghettini, holding it straight up like a bunch of flowers and gently pushing it into the water as it softens. Add a tablespoon of salt and give the pasta a quick stir. Briefly put the lid on until it starts to lift, showing that the water has come back to a boil, then let the pasta bubble away, uncovered, for about 8 minutes, or until it is tender but still has some bite to it.

4 Meanwhile, drain the tofu, reserving the marinade. Heat a little peanut oil in a frying pan and fry the pieces of tofu for a minute or two on each side, until browned and crisp. Drain the tofu on paper towels and keep it warm.

5 Drain the pasta by tipping it all into a colander placed in the sink, then put it back into the still-warm pan with the sesame oil, scallions, peanuts, reserved marinade and black pepper to taste. Mix gently, then serve on warm plates, topped with the tofu and generous amounts of cilantro.

PIPE RIGATE WITH RED PEPPERS AND GARLIC Serves ❹

INGREDIENTS

4 red bell peppers

14 ounces pipe rigate

salt

2 fat juicy garlic cloves, peeled and thinly sliced

2 Tbs olive oil

freshly ground black pepper

fresh basil leaves, to serve

As an alternative to broiling the peppers, you could roast them in the oven, as described on page 58. They can be done well ahead of time, when convenient, and reheated just before you want to use them.

1 First fill a large saucepan with 4 quarts of water and bring to a boil over high heat for the pasta.

2 Next prepare the peppers by cutting them into quarters and placing, skin-side (shiny side) up, on a broiler pan. Put under high heat for 10–15 minutes, until the skin has blistered and blackened in places. Cover the peppers with a plate and leave until cool enough to handle, then remove the skin, stem and seeds, and cut the flesh into strips.

3 When the water in the saucepan boils, add the pasta along with a tablespoon of salt and give the pasta a quick stir. Briefly put the lid on until it starts to lift, showing that the water has come back to a boil, then let the pasta bubble away, uncovered, for about 8 minutes, or until it is tender but still has some bite to it.

4 Meanwhile, sauté the garlic in the olive oil over low heat for 2–3 minutes, without letting it brown. Keep on one side.

5 Drain the pasta by tipping it all into a colander placed in the sink, then put it back into the still-warm pan. Add the olive oil and garlic to the pasta, along with the pepper strips, toss gently, add salt and pepper to taste and serve on warm plates, tearing basil over the top.

WHOLE WHEAT FUSILLI WITH GOAT CHEESE, SUN-DRIED TOMATOES AND BASIL Serves ❹

INGREDIENTS

14 ounces whole wheat fusilli

salt

1 Tbs olive oil or oil from the sun-dried tomatoes

8 sun-dried tomatoes, chopped

8 ounces goat cheese, diced or broken into small pieces

freshly torn basil leaves

freshly ground black pepper

The nutty flavor of whole wheat fusilli is a good foil for the intense goat cheese and sun-dried tomatoes in this recipe.

1 First fill a large saucepan with 4 quarts of water and bring to a boil over high heat for the pasta.

2 When the water boils, add the pasta along with a tablespoon of salt and give the pasta a quick stir. Briefly put the lid on until it starts to lift, showing that the water has come back to a boil, then let the pasta bubble away, uncovered, for about 8 minutes, or until it is tender but still has some bite to it.

3 Drain the pasta by tipping it all into a colander placed in the sink, then put it back into the still-warm pan, add the olive oil, sun-dried tomatoes, goat cheese, basil and salt and pepper to taste. Toss gently and serve on warm plates.

FUSILLI WITH CHILI, LEEKS AND ZUCCHINI Serves ❹

INGREDIENTS

olive oil

8 ounces leeks, trimmed and cut into ¼-inch slices

1 fresh green chili, de-seeded and chopped

8 ounces zucchini, trimmed and cut into matchsticks

14 ounces fusilli

salt and freshly ground black pepper

freshly grated pecorino cheese, to serve

This succulent mixture of pasta, leeks and zucchini is enlivened with chili – add more or less, according to your taste.

1 First fill a large saucepan with 4 quarts of water and bring to a boil over high heat for the pasta.

2 Meanwhile, heat 4 tablespoons of olive oil in a saucepan and put in the leeks and chili. Cover and cook slowly for 6–8 minutes, until the leeks are beginning to soften, then put in the zucchini and cook for a further 3–4 minutes, until the zucchini and leeks are tender. Keep the mixture warm.

3 When the water in the saucepan boils, add the pasta along with a tablespoon of salt and give the pasta a quick stir. Briefly put the lid on until it starts to lift, showing that the water has come back to a boil, then let the pasta bubble away, uncovered, for about 8 minutes, or until it is tender but still has some bite to it.

4 Drain the pasta by tipping it all into a colander placed in the sink, then put it back into the still-warm pan, add the leek mixture, season with salt and black pepper as necessary and toss gently. Serve on warm plates, and pass the pecorino separately.

PENNE RIGATE WITH TOMATOES, BASIL, PINE NUTS AND CHILI Serves ❹

INGREDIENTS

2 Tbs olive oil

2 pounds fresh tomatoes, skinned and chopped

2 fat juicy garlic cloves, peeled and thinly sliced

1 fresh green chili, de-seeded and finely sliced

14 ounces penne rigate

salt

¼–½ cup pine nuts

4 good sprigs of fresh basil leaves, torn

freshly ground black pepper

I think of this as a summer dish – it is at its best when made with flavorful, juicy, plum tomatoes – but it can also bring some sunny warmth to a wintry day, made with whatever fresh tomatoes are available and a good kick of chili added.

1 First fill a large saucepan with 4 quarts of water and bring to a boil over high heat for the pasta.

2 Meanwhile, heat the olive oil in a saucepan and put in the tomatoes, garlic and chili. Cook slowly, covered, for 10–15 minutes, until the tomatoes have collapsed.

3 When the water in the saucepan boils, add the pasta along with a tablespoon of salt and give the pasta a quick stir. Briefly put the lid on until it starts to lift, showing that the water has come back to a boil, then let the

pasta bubble away, uncovered, for about 8 minutes, or until it is tender but still has some bite to it.

4 Drain the pasta by tipping it all into a colander placed in the sink, then put it back into the still-warm pan and add the tomato mixture, pine nuts and basil. Toss gently, season with salt and pepper, and serve on warm plates.

NOODLES WITH SNOW PEAS, WATER CHESTNUTS AND CORN Serves ❹

INGREDIENTS

2 Tbs peanut oil

2 garlic cloves, peeled and crushed

1 tsp grated fresh ginger

1½ cups snow peas, trimmed and sliced diagonally

4 ounces baby corn, sliced diagonally

⅓ cup sliced canned water chestnuts, drained

4 scallions, trimmed and sliced diagonally

14 ounces Chinese noodles

2 Tbs soy sauce, such as Kikkoman

salt and freshly ground black pepper

fresh cilantro leaves, to serve

The delicious water chestnut is eaten fresh in Asia and available in cans here. Its crunchy texture contrasts well with the soft texture of the noodles. The noodles make this a very quick dish to prepare, since all they need is a brief soaking before being combined with the other ingredients. You could use other vegetables instead of the ones I have suggested – broccoli florets, red, yellow or green bell peppers or young green beans, for instance.

1 Heat the oil in a large saucepan and put in the garlic and ginger. Stir for 30 seconds, then add the snow peas, corn, water chestnuts and scallions and stir-fry for 2–3 minutes, until the mixture is heated through.

2 Meanwhile, bring a saucepan of water to a boil. Put the noodles into a large bowl, cover generously with boiling water and leave for 2–3 minutes (or according to the instructions on the package) until tender, then drain them.

3 Add the noodles to the snow pea mixture in the saucepan, along with the soy sauce and salt and pepper as necessary, stir quickly over the heat and then serve immediately on warm plates. Tear some cilantro leaves over the top.

FUSILLI LUNGHI WITH CHERRY TOMATOES, GREEN BELL PEPPERS AND CAPERS Serves ❹

INGREDIENTS

2 Tbs olive oil

2 green bell peppers, de-seeded and chopped

1 fat juicy garlic clove, peeled and sliced

3 cups cherry tomatoes, halved

14 ounces fusilli lunghi

salt

2 Tbs capers

2 Tbs freshly torn flat-leaf parsley

freshly ground black pepper

Pretty and piquant, this pasta dish makes the most of sweet cherry tomatoes. For an even more colorful effect, include some yellow cherry tomatoes in the mixture.

1 First fill a large saucepan with 4 quarts of water and bring to a boil over high heat for the pasta.

2 Meanwhile, heat the oil in a saucepan, put in the bell peppers and garlic, cover and cook gently for about 15 minutes, until the peppers are tender, stirring from time to time. Then add the cherry tomatoes, cover and cook lightly for about 5 minutes.

3 When the water in the saucepan boils, add the pasta along with a tablespoon of salt and give the pasta a quick stir. Briefly put the lid on until it starts to lift, showing that the water has come back to a boil, then let the pasta bubble away, uncovered, for about 8 minutes, or until it is tender but still has some bite to it.

4 Drain the pasta by tipping it all into a colander placed in the sink, then put it back into the still-warm pan and add the green pepper and tomato mixture, the capers, the parsley, and salt and pepper to taste. Toss gently and serve on warm plates.

PENNONI WITH CROUTONS AND CARAMELIZED ONIONS Serves ❹

INGREDIENTS

olive oil

1½ pounds onions, preferably red, peeled and sliced

14 ounces pennoni

salt

4 slices of bread, crusts removed

freshly ground black pepper

freshly grated Parmesan cheese, to serve

This surprisingly good combination of textures and flavors can also be served with farfalle, or any other chunky pasta. The important thing is to give the onions long enough to cook, so that they become meltingly tender and sweet.

1 First cook the onions. Heat 2 tablespoons of oil in a pan, add the onions, stir, then cover and leave over low heat for 30 minutes, until very tender. Stir from time to time, especially toward the end, so they do not stick.

2 Fill a large saucepan with 4 quarts of water and bring to a boil over high heat for the pasta.

3 When the water in the saucepan boils, add the pasta along with a tablespoon of salt and give the pasta a quick stir. Briefly put the lid on until it starts to lift, showing that the water has come back to a boil, then let the pasta bubble away, uncovered, for about 8 minutes, or until it is tender but still has some bite to it.

4 Meanwhile, make the croutons. Fry the bread on both sides in a little hot olive oil, until crisp and golden. Cut into small squares and keep on one side.

5 Drain the pasta by tipping it all into a colander placed in the sink, then put it back into the still-warm pan and add the onions. Toss gently, season with salt and pepper and serve on warm plates, scattering the croutons on top. Parmesan goes well with this – pass it around separately.

RIGATONI WITH RED BELL PEPPERS, SPINACH AND LENTILS Serves ❹

INGREDIENTS

2 large red bell peppers

14 ounces rigatoni

salt

3 cups tender spinach, washed

2 Tbs olive oil

½ cup brown or green lentils, cooked, or a 14-ounce can

squeeze of lemon juice

freshly ground black pepper

If you are using dry lentils, cook them first (no need to soak) in plenty of water until tender. This takes about 30 to 50 minutes, depending on the lentils, so keep checking them toward the end of their cooking time.

1 First prepare the bell peppers by cutting them into quarters and placing, skin-side (shiny side) up, on a broiler pan. Put under high heat for 10–15 minutes, until the skin has blistered and blackened in places. Cover the peppers with a plate and leave until cool enough to handle, then remove the skin, stem and seeds, and cut the flesh into strips.

2 Fill a large saucepan with 4 quarts of water and bring to a boil over high heat for the pasta.

3 When the water in the saucepan boils, add the pasta along with a tablespoon of salt and give the pasta a quick stir. Briefly put the lid on until it starts to lift, showing that the water has come back to a boil, then let the pasta bubble away, uncovered, for about 8 minutes, or until it is tender but still has some bite to it.

4 Meanwhile, dry the spinach leaves on paper towels and cook in 1 tablespoon of the olive oil in a large saucepan for 2–3 minutes, or until it is just wilted. Add the lentils and their liquid and heat gently. Add a dash of lemon juice to taste and season with salt and pepper.

5 Drain the pasta by tipping it all into a colander placed in the sink, then put it back into the still-warm pan. Either add the remaining olive oil to the pasta, serve it on warm plates and put the spinach mixture and the peppers on top; or add all of these to the pasta, toss gently and serve immediately on warm plates.

FUSILLI LUNGHI WITH BROCCOLI, BROILED RED AND YELLOW BELL PEPPERS AND OLIVES Serves ❹

INGREDIENTS

1 large red bell pepper

1 large yellow bell pepper

14 ounces fusilli lunghi

salt

3 cups broccoli florets, cut into even-sized pieces

1 Tbs olive oil

⅓ cup black olives

freshly ground black pepper

fresh basil leaves and flakes of Parmesan cheese, to serve

Vibrant colors and intense flavors combine to make this an attractive dish. Broil the bell peppers well in advance, if you like, to save time later. If the peppers are to be served the same day, do not refrigerate them.

1 First prepare the peppers by cutting them into quarters and placing, skin-side (shiny side) up, on a broiler pan. Put under high heat for 10–15 minutes, until the skin has blistered and blackened in places. Cover the peppers with a plate and leave until cool enough to handle, then remove the skin, stem and seeds, and cut the flesh into strips.

2 Next fill a large saucepan with 4 quarts of water and bring to a boil over high heat for the pasta.

3 When the water in the saucepan boils, add the pasta along with a tablespoon of salt and give the pasta a quick stir. Briefly put the lid on until it starts to lift, showing that the water has come back to a boil, then let the pasta bubble away, uncovered, for about 8 minutes, or until it is tender but still has some bite to it.

4 Meanwhile, cook the broccoli in a little boiling water for about 4 minutes, or until tender. Drain and keep warm.

5 Drain the pasta by tipping it all into a colander placed in the sink, then put it back into the still-warm pan with the olive oil, pepper strips, broccoli, olives and salt and pepper to taste. Stir gently, then serve the pasta on warm plates. Tear the basil over and scatter the Parmesan on top.

RIGATONI WITH MUSHROOMS, LEEKS AND SUN-DRIED TOMATOES Serves ❹

INGREDIENTS

1½ cups leeks, trimmed and cut into
¼ inch slices

olive oil

14 ounces rigatoni

salt

2 cups mushrooms, cleaned
and sliced

2 garlic cloves, peeled and crushed

8 sun-dried tomatoes, chopped

freshly ground black pepper

This is good just as it is, or it can be embellished with some chopped or torn parsley or basil and either Parmesan or pecorino cheese.

1 First fill a large saucepan with 4 quarts of water and bring to a boil over high heat for the pasta.

2 Meanwhile, cook the leeks either in a little boiling water or in 2–3 tablespoons of olive oil, with a lid on the pan, for 8–10 minutes until tender. Drain (if cooked in water) and keep warm.

3 When the water in the saucepan boils, add the pasta along with a tablespoon of salt and give the pasta a quick stir. Briefly put the lid on until it starts to lift, showing that the water has come back to a boil, then let the pasta bubble away, uncovered, for about 8 minutes, or until it is tender but still has some bite to it.

4 Fry the mushrooms in 2 tablespoons of olive oil, with the garlic, for 4–5 minutes, until tender and any liquid has boiled away. Mix together the leeks, mushrooms and sun-dried tomatoes, and season with salt and pepper.

5 Drain the pasta by tipping it all into a colander placed in the sink, then put it back into the still-warm pan. Either add a tablespoon of olive oil to the pasta, serve it on plates and spoon the leek mixture on top; or add the leek mixture directly to the pasta, toss gently and serve on warm plates.

LUMACHE WITH FETA CHEESE AND BROCCOLI Serves ❹

INGREDIENTS

14 ounces lumache

salt

4 cups prepared broccoli, cut
into ½ inch pieces

1 Tbs olive oil

4 ounces feta cheese

freshly ground black pepper

fresh basil leaves, to serve

There are lovely Mediterranean flavors in this simple pasta dish.

1 First fill a large saucepan with 4 quarts of water and bring to a boil over high heat for the pasta.

2 When the water boils, add the pasta along with a tablespoon of salt and give the pasta a quick stir. Briefly put the lid on until it starts to lift, showing that the water has come back to a boil, then let the pasta bubble away, uncovered, for about 8 minutes, or until it is tender but still has some bite to it.

3 Meanwhile, cook the broccoli in a little boiling water for 3–4 minutes, or until it is just tender, then drain the broccoli and keep it warm.

4 Drain the pasta by tipping it all into a colander placed in the sink, then put it back into the still-warm pan with the olive oil, stirring gently so that the olive oil coats the pasta. Then add the feta and broccoli, check the seasoning, toss gently and serve on warm plates. Tear the basil over the top.

PIPE RIGATE WITH EGGPLANT, RICOTTA AND BASIL Serves ❹

INGREDIENTS

2 eggplants, sliced then cut across into smaller pieces

salt

olive oil

2 fat juicy garlic cloves, peeled and sliced

freshly ground black pepper

14 ounces pipe rigate

1 cup ricotta cheese

4 good sprigs of fresh basil leaves, torn

A wonderful contrast of different textures feature in this dish. Remember to allow an hour's salting time for the eggplants.

1 Put the eggplant pieces into a colander, sprinkle with salt and leave for an hour to draw out any bitter juices and also prevent the eggplant from absorbing too much oil when you fry it. Then rinse the eggplant under cold water and squeeze it dry.

2 Fill a large saucepan with 4 quarts of water and bring to a boil over high heat for the pasta.

3 Heat 3 tablespoons of olive oil in a saucepan, put in the eggplant pieces and the garlic, stir, cover and leave to cook gently for about 20 minutes until the eggplant is

tender. Stir the eggplant from time to time to prevent it from sticking. Season with salt and black pepper.

4 When the water in the saucepan boils, add the pasta along with a tablespoon of salt and give the pasta a quick stir. Briefly put the lid on until it starts to lift, showing that the water has come back to a boil, then let the pasta bubble away, uncovered, for about 8 minutes, or until it is tender but still has some bite to it.

5 Drain the pasta by tipping it all into a colander placed in the sink, then put it back into the still-warm pan. Mix the ricotta in roughly with a fork, so that it is lumpy, then add the eggplant and basil. Toss gently, check the seasoning and serve on warm plates.

PENNONI WITH BROCCOLI, MASCARPONE, GARLIC AND FRESH BASIL Serves ❹

INGREDIENTS

14 ounces pennoni

salt

4 cups prepared broccoli, cut into ½ inch pieces

1 garlic clove, peeled and crushed

1 Tbs olive oil

½ cup mascarpone cheese

freshly ground black pepper

fresh basil leaves, to serve

The mascarpone cheese gives this recipe a delectable creaminess but could be replaced with a low-fat smooth white cheese.

1 First fill a large saucepan with 4 quarts of water and bring to a boil over high heat for the pasta.

2 When the water boils, add the pasta along with a tablespoon of salt and give the pasta a quick stir. Briefly put the lid on until it starts to lift, showing that the water has come back to a boil, then let the pasta bubble away, uncovered, for about 8 minutes, or until it is tender but still has some bite to it.

3 Meanwhile, cook the broccoli in a little boiling water for 3–4 minutes, or until just tender, then drain and keep warm.

4 Cook the garlic in the olive oil over low heat for 2–3 minutes, without letting it brown. Keep on one side.

5 Drain the pasta by tipping it all into a colander placed in the sink, then put it back into the still-warm pan with the garlic, along with its oil, stirring gently so that the oil coats the pasta. Add the mascarpone cheese and broccoli, season, toss gently and serve on warm plates. Tear the basil over the top.

FARFALLE WITH CARROTS, GOAT CHEESE, THYME AND SUN-DRIED TOMATOES Serves ❹

INGREDIENTS

14 ounces farfalle

salt

2 large carrots, scraped

8 sun-dried tomatoes, chopped

4 good sprigs of thyme,
leaves crumbled

1 Tbs olive oil or oil from
the sun-dried tomatoes

8 ounces goat cheese, diced or
broken into small pieces

freshly ground black pepper

An unusual combination of ingredients that works really well – try it! You can use either a soft white goat cheese log or the kind with a rind.

1 First fill a large saucepan with 4 quarts of water and bring to a boil over high heat for the pasta.

2 When the water boils, add the pasta along with a tablespoon of salt and give the pasta a quick stir. Briefly put the lid on until it starts to lift, showing that the water has come back to a boil, then let the pasta bubble away, uncovered, for about 8 minutes, or until it is tender but still has some bite to it.

3 Meanwhile, heat another, smaller pan with water for the carrots. Grate the carrots, then cook them for 1 minute in the pan of water. Drain and return to the pan with the sun-dried tomatoes and thyme. Keep warm.

4 Drain the pasta by tipping it all into a colander placed in the sink, then put it back into the still-warm pan, add the olive or sun-dried tomato oil, carrot mixture and goat cheese, with salt and pepper to taste. Toss gently and serve on warm plates.

PENNE WITH RED ONIONS, GOAT CHEESE AND WALNUTS Serves ❹

INGREDIENTS

2 Tbs olive oil

1½ pounds red onions, peeled and thinly sliced

14 ounces penne

salt

4 ounces smooth goat cheese, roughly chopped

⅓ cup shelled walnuts, preferably freshly cracked

freshly ground black pepper

A nice autumn mixture, making the most of new season walnuts and the strong flavors of red onions and goat cheese. If you do not like goat cheese, you could use any smooth white creamy cheese instead.

1 First get the onions cooking. Heat the olive oil in a saucepan, put in the onions, stir, then cover and leave over low heat for 30 minutes, until very tender. Stir from time to time, especially toward the end, to make sure they do not stick.

2 Next, fill a large saucepan with 4 quarts of water and bring to a boil over high heat for the pasta.

3 When the water boils, add the pasta along with a tablespoon of salt and give the pasta a quick stir. Briefly put the lid on until it starts to lift, showing that the water has come back to a boil, then let the pasta bubble away, uncovered, for about 8 minutes, or until it is tender but still has some bite to it.

4 Drain the pasta by tipping it all into a colander placed in the sink, then put it back into the still-warm pan, add the goat cheese and toss gently. Then add the onions and walnuts, and salt and pepper to taste, and serve on warm plates.

PIPE RIGATE WITH SWISS CHARD, MASCARPONE AND PINE NUTS Serves ❹

INGREDIENTS

1 pound Swiss chard, washed

2 Tbs olive oil

salt and freshly ground black pepper

14 ounces pipe rigate

½ cup mascarpone cheese

½ cup pine nuts, toasted (see page 78)

Swiss chard is delicious if you can get it; if not, use tender spinach instead, cooking it for just 2–3 minutes until wilted.

1 First fill a large saucepan with 4 quarts of water and bring to a boil over high heat for the pasta.

2 Separate the leafy part of the Swiss chard from the stems. Cut the stems into ½ inch lengths, then gently cook in the olive oil for about 7 minutes until just tender. Add the leafy parts and cook for a further 4 minutes or until these are tender, too. Season with salt and pepper.

3 When the water boils, add the pasta along with a tablespoon of salt and give the pasta a quick stir. Briefly put the lid on until it starts to lift, showing that the water has come back to a boil, then let the pasta bubble away, uncovered, for about 8 minutes, or until it is tender but still has some bite to it.

4 Drain the pasta by tipping it all into a colander placed in the sink, then put it back into the still-warm pan, add the Swiss chard, mascarpone and pine nuts, toss gently and serve on warm plates.

VERMICELLI WITH CHICKPEAS Serves ❹

INGREDIENTS

2 14-ounce cans chickpeas

14 ounces vermicelli

salt

2–4 Tbs olive oil

2 garlic cloves, peeled and crushed

freshly ground black pepper

1–2 Tbs chopped fresh parsley, optional

2 Tbs sesame seeds, toasted (see page 78), to serve

This is a classic Italian dish known as *tuono e lampo* – "thunder and lightning," which refers to the contrasting textures of the pasta and chickpeas.

1 Put the chickpeas, together with their liquid, into a saucepan and heat gently.

2 Next fill a large saucepan with 4 quarts of water and bring to a boil over high heat for the pasta.

3 When the water boils, add the pasta along with a tablespoon of salt and give the pasta a quick stir. Briefly put the lid on until it starts to lift, showing that the water has come back to a boil, then cook the vermicelli, uncovered, for 3–4 minutes, or until it is tender but still has some bite to it, stirring all the time so that the thin strands do not stick together.

4 Drain the pasta by tipping it all into a colander placed in the sink, then put it back into the still-warm pan with 2–4 tablespoons of olive oil, to your taste, the garlic and a few grindings of pepper.

5 Add the chickpeas to the pasta, toss gently and serve on warmed plates. Sprinkle with the parsley, if using, and the sesame seeds.

VEGETABLE CHOW MEIN Serves ❹

INGREDIENTS

2 Tbs roasted sesame oil

8 scallions, trimmed and sliced

1 garlic clove, peeled and crushed

1 red bell pepper, de-seeded and chopped

4 ounces baby corn, cut into ½-inch lengths

1 cup mushrooms, cleaned and sliced

1 Tbs cornstarch

2 Tbs soy sauce

2 Tbs sherry

⅔ cup vegetable stock

14 ounces vermicelli

salt

1 Tbs olive oil

1–2 Tbs sesame seeds

This is good as a main course on its own or as part of a Chinese meal along with some stir-fried vegetables and boiled rice. Hand around soy sauce at the table for people to add more if they wish.

1 First fill a large saucepan with 4 quarts of water and bring to a boil over high heat for the pasta.

2 Meanwhile, heat the sesame oil in a large saucepan and put in the scallions, garlic, red bell pepper, corn and mushrooms. Sauté for 5 minutes, stirring often.

3 Put the cornstarch into a small bowl or cup and add the soy sauce, sherry and vegetable stock. Pour this mixture into the saucepan with the vegetable mixture, bring to a boil and cook for 1 minute, stirring. Remove from the heat and leave on one side while you cook the pasta.

4 When the water in the saucepan boils, add the pasta along with a tablespoon of salt and give the pasta a quick stir. Briefly put the lid on until it starts to lift, showing that the water has come back to a boil, then cook the vermicelli, uncovered, for 3–4 minutes, or until it is tender but still has some bite to it, stirring all the time so that the thin strands do not stick together.

5 Drain the pasta by tipping it all into a colander placed in the sink, then put it back into the still-warm pan with the olive oil. Stir gently and leave on one side.

6 Quickly reheat the vegetable mixture, then pour it in with the pasta. Toss gently, serve on warmed plates and sprinkle with the sesame seeds.

The Classic Sauces

Here you will find five classic sauces, each followed by recipes that add other ingredients to create a variety of different dishes. Once you have made the basic sauce, you have many possibilities before you. Three of the basic sauces – tomato, béchamel and lentil bolognese – freeze very well, so it can be helpful to make a double quantity and put one batch away in the freezer for another day. The pesto and cream sauces keep well, tightly covered, in the refrigerator – pesto for up to two weeks, cream sauce for a couple of days.

While pesto, cream sauce, béchamel and tomato sauce are all indisputably "classic," you might think I am stretching things a bit when I include in this section lentil bolognese sauce. I have included it because, while it may not be a classic sauce in the same sense that the others are, it is definitely a classic as far as vegetarian cooking is concerned, and a most useful and nutritious sauce as well. If you want something filling to keep the chill out on a winter's night, then this is the one for you.

Béchamel sauce fell into disrepute for a time in foodie circles a few years ago, perhaps because it was overused in recipes where a lighter touch would have been preferable. However, it is certainly a classic sauce, and delicious if well made. Like other recipes in this book that contain milk or cream, béchamel sauce can be very satisfactorily made with soy milk and cream and, indeed, these are what I prefer to use instead of dairy milk.

PESTO Serves ❹

INGREDIENTS

2 cups fresh basil leaves

2 garlic cloves, peeled

2 Tbs pine nuts, toasted

½ cup olive oil

⅓ cup freshly grated Parmesan cheese, optional

salt and freshly ground black pepper

squeeze of lemon juice, optional

• VARIATION •
LOW-FAT PESTO

Replace 4 tablespoons of the oil with very low-fat fromage blanc, or, to reduce calories further, with water.

Recipes for classic pesto sauce vary slightly and some people argue details but, quite honestly, when a recipe contains basil, garlic, olive oil, pine nuts and Parmesan you really cannot go wrong! It is also a basic idea that can be successfully adapted in a number of ways, as the following recipes show.

1 Put the basil leaves, garlic cloves and pine nuts into a food processor or blender, with a little of the olive oil if necessary for the machine to work, and whizz to a fairly smooth paste. (A blender needs a little liquid in order to work, while a food processor can often start off with "dry" ingredients.)

2 Gradually add the rest of the oil, whizzing as you go, then transfer the mixture to a bowl, or to a screw-top jar if you are planning to keep the pesto in the refrigerator. Stir in the Parmesan cheese, if using.

3 Season with salt and pepper and add a squeeze of lemon juice to bring out the flavor if you think it needs it. Either use immediately, adding the pesto directly to hot, cooked spaghetti, tagliatelle or other pasta, or keep it in the refrigerator for up to 2 weeks.

•

A jar of pesto keeps well in the refrigerator. Besides being wonderful on pasta it is great on bread: spread it on slices of bread and broil or bake. You can also top baked potatoes with pesto, and add it to a simple béchamel sauce as well as to vegetable and pasta soups and pasta bakes.

You can make pesto in the traditional way using a mortar and pestle if you like. It takes longer, but the method is the same, with elbow power replacing the action of a machine.

For how to toast pine nuts, see page 78.

PENNE WITH CHILI PESTO Serves ❹

INGREDIENTS

14 ounces penne

salt

FOR THE PESTO:

2 cups fresh basil leaves

2 garlic cloves, peeled

2 Tbs pine nuts, toasted

1–2 fresh green chilies, de-seeded

½ cup olive oil

salt and freshly ground black pepper

squeeze of lemon juice, optional

Fresh chili gives a kick to this pesto: add it judiciously, according to the type of chilies you are using and to your taste. You may prefer to chop the chili finely and stir it in at the end, bit by bit, until you get your desired degree of heat.

1 First fill a large saucepan with 4 quarts of water and bring to a boil over high heat for the pasta.

2 Meanwhile, make the pesto – or this can be done well in advance if you prefer. Follow the recipe above, pulverizing the chilies along with the basil leaves and the other ingredients and leaving out the Parmesan cheese.

3 When the water boils, add the pasta along with a tablespoon of salt and give the pasta a quick stir. Briefly put the lid on until it starts to lift, showing that the water has come back to a boil, then let the pasta bubble away, uncovered, for about 8 minutes, or until it is tender but still has some bite to it.

4 Reserve about a cup of water from the pasta. Drain the pasta by tipping it all into a colander placed in the sink, then put it back into the still-warm pan. Stir the pesto and loosen it a bit, if it needs it, by adding a couple of tablespoons of the pasta water, then add it to the pasta. Toss the pasta gently until well coated with the pesto, check the seasoning, then serve at once on warm plates.

SPAGHETTI WITH CILANTRO AND CHILI PESTO WITH RED BELL PEPPER Serves ❹

INGREDIENTS

14 ounces spaghetti

salt

½ red bell pepper, de-seeded and finely chopped. to serve

FOR THE PESTO:

2 cups fresh cilantro leaves

2 garlic cloves, peeled

1 dried red chili, crumbled

2 Tbs pine nuts, toasted

½ cup olive oil

salt and freshly ground black pepper

squeeze of lemon juice, optional

Cilantro makes a pesto with a difference and the flecks of red chili look pretty and add their own punch – you may not need much, depending on your taste.

1 First fill a large saucepan with 4 quarts of water and bring to a boil over high heat for the pasta.

2 Meanwhile, make the pesto – or this can be done well in advance if you prefer. Follow the recipe, opposite, using cilantro instead of basil, adding the chili with the garlic and leaving out the Parmesan cheese.

3 When the water in the saucepan boils, add the spaghetti, holding it straight up like a bunch of flowers and gently pushing it into the water as it softens. Add a tablespoon of salt and give the pasta a quick stir. Briefly put the lid on until it starts to lift, showing that the water has come back to a boil, then let the pasta bubble away, uncovered, for about 8 minutes, or until it is tender but still has some bite to it.

4 Scoop up about a cup of water from the pasta and set aside. Drain the pasta by tipping it all into a colander placed in the sink, then put it back into the still-warm pan. Loosen the pesto, if it needs it, by mixing in a couple of tablespoons of the pasta water, then add it to the pasta. Toss the pasta gently until well coated, check the seasoning, then serve at once on warm plates, and sprinkle with the chopped red bell pepper.

PENNE WITH SUN-DRIED TOMATO PESTO, FRESH BASIL AND PARMESAN Serves ❹

INGREDIENTS

14 ounces penne

salt

fresh basil leaves and flakes of Parmesan cheese, to serve

FOR THE PESTO:

2 ounces sun-dried tomatoes

2 garlic cloves, peeled

2 Tbs pine nuts, toasted

½ cup oil – from the tomatoes plus olive oil to make up

salt and freshly ground black pepper

squeeze of lemon juice, optional

There's a lovely sunny mixture of flavors in this unusual pesto. Use sun-dried tomatoes in oil and drain before weighing.

1 First fill a large saucepan with 4 quarts of water and bring to a boil over high heat.

2 Meanwhile, make the pesto – or this can be done in advance. Follow recipe, opposite, using sun-dried tomatoes instead of basil.

3 When the water boils, add the pasta along with a tablespoon of salt and give the pasta a quick stir. Briefly put the lid on until it starts to lift, showing that the water has come back to a boil, then let the pasta bubble away, uncovered, for about 8 minutes, or until it is tender but still has some bite to it.

4 Reserve a cup of water from the pasta. Drain the pasta by tipping it all into a colander placed in the sink, then put it back into the still-warm pan. Loosen the pesto a bit, if it needs it, by mixing in a couple of tablespoons of the pasta water, then add it to the pasta. Toss the pasta gently to coat well, check the seasoning, then serve at once on warm plates, tearing basil over the top and scattering with Parmesan.

SPAGHETTI WITH CHILI—RED-PEPPER PESTO Serves ❹

INGREDIENTS

14 ounces spaghetti

salt

fresh basil leaves, to serve, optional

FOR THE PESTO:

1 red bell pepper

2 garlic cloves, peeled

2 Tbs pine nuts, toasted

1 dried red chili, optional

½ cup olive oil

salt and freshly ground black pepper

squeeze of lemon juice, optional

Scarlet and warming, chili–red-pepper pesto goes well with most of the more substantial pastas, and with tagliatelle and penne too.

1 First prepare the bell pepper for the pesto by cutting it into quarters and placing, skin-side (shiny-side) up, on a broiler pan. Put under a high heat for 10–15 minutes, until the skin has blistered and blackened in places. Cover the pepper with a plate and leave until cool enough to handle, then remove the skin, stem and seeds, and cut the flesh into slices.

2 Next fill a large saucepan with 4 quarts of water and bring to a boil over high heat for the pasta.

3 Meanwhile, make the pesto – or this can be done well in advance if you prefer. Follow the recipe on page 76, using the red bell pepper instead of the basil, adding the red chili, if using, and leaving out the Parmesan.

4 When the water in the saucepan boils, add the spaghetti, holding it straight up like a bunch of flowers and gently pushing it into the water as it softens. Add a tablespoon of salt and give the pasta a quick stir. Briefly put the lid on until it starts to lift, showing that the water has come back to a boil, then let the pasta bubble away, uncovered, for about 8 minutes, or until it is tender but still has some bite to it.

5 Reserve about a cup of water from the pasta. Drain the pasta by tipping it all into a colander placed in the sink, then put it back into the still-warm pan. Give the pesto a stir and loosen it a bit, if it needs it, by mixing in a couple of tablespoons of the pasta water, then add it to the pasta. Toss the pasta gently until it is all coated with the pesto, check the seasoning, then serve at once on warm plates. Tear some basil leaves over the top if you like.

•

To toast pine nuts, spread them out in a single layer on a cookie sheet and put under a hot broiler until they turn golden brown and smell toasted. This will happen very quickly, in a minute or two, so do not take your eyes off them. Give them a stir halfway through so that both sides get toasted evenly. Other nuts, such as walnuts, pecans or flaked almonds, can be toasted in the same way. So too can sesame seeds, but they take only seconds.

SPAGHETTI WITH OLIVE PESTO Serves ❹

INGREDIENTS

14 ounces spaghetti

salt

fresh basil or flat-leaf parsley, to serve

FOR THE PESTO:

½ cup pitted black olives

2 garlic cloves, peeled

2 Tbs pine nuts, toasted (see page 78)

1 dried red chili, optional

½ cup olive oil

salt and freshly ground black pepper

squeeze of lemon juice, optional

This is a rich-tasting pesto in which the flavor of the olives really comes out. A mixed salad of lettuce, tomato and basil goes well with it, and some warm bread.

1 First fill a large saucepan with 4 quarts of water and bring to a boil over high heat for the pasta.

2 Meanwhile, make the pesto – or this can be done well in advance if you prefer. Follow the recipe on page 76, using the olives instead of the basil, adding the chili, if using, with the other ingredients and leaving out the Parmesan.

3 When the water in the saucepan boils, add the spaghetti, holding it straight up like a bunch of flowers and gently pushing it into the water as it softens. Add a tablespoon of salt and give the pasta a quick stir. Briefly put the lid on until it starts to lift, showing that the water has come back to a boil, then let the pasta bubble away, uncovered, for about 8 minutes, or until it is tender but still has some bite to it.

4 Reserve about a cup of water from the pasta. Drain the pasta by tipping it all into a colander placed in the sink, then put it back into the still-warm pan. Stir the pesto and loosen it a bit, if it needs it, by mixing in a couple of tablespoons of the hot pasta water, then add it to the pasta. Toss the pasta gently until it is all coated with the pesto, check the seasoning, then serve at once on warm plates. Tear or snip basil or flat-leaf parsley over the top.

CONCHIGLIE WITH PARSLEY PESTO AND ARTICHOKE HEARTS Serves ❹

INGREDIENTS

14 ounces conchiglie

salt

14 ounces canned artichoke hearts, drained and sliced

FOR THE PESTO:

2 cups fresh parsley leaves

2 garlic cloves, peeled

2 Tbs pine nuts, toasted (see page 78)

½ cup olive oil

⅔ cup freshly grated Parmesan

salt and freshly ground black pepper

squeeze of lemon juice, optional

You can use either curly parsley or flat-leaf parsley for this pesto. I generally use canned artichoke hearts, because I like them and they do not have any added fat, but you could use a jar of artichokes in oil if you prefer.

1 First fill a large saucepan with 4 quarts of water and bring to a boil over high heat for the pasta.

2 Meanwhile, make the pesto – or this can be done well in advance if you prefer. Follow the recipe on page 76, using parsley instead of basil.

3 When the water boils, add the pasta along with a tablespoon of salt and give the pasta a quick stir. Briefly put the lid on until it starts to lift, showing that the water has come back to a boil, then let the pasta bubble away, uncovered, for about 8 minutes, or until it is tender but still has some bite to it.

4 Reserve about a cup of water from the pasta. Drain the pasta by tipping it all into a colander placed in the sink, then put it back into the still-warm pan. Give the pesto a stir and loosen it a bit, if it needs it, by mixing in a couple of tablespoons of the reserved hot pasta water, then add it to the pasta. Toss the pasta gently until it is all coated with the pesto, then add the sliced artichoke hearts. Check the seasoning, and serve at once on warm plates.

FETTUCCINE WITH MINT PESTO AND PEAS Serves ❹

INGREDIENTS

14 ounces fettuccine

salt

1½ cups shelled fresh peas or frozen petits pois

FOR THE PESTO:

2 cups fresh mint leaves

2 garlic cloves, peeled

2 Tbs pine nuts, toasted (see page 78)

½ cup olive oil

salt and freshly ground black pepper

squeeze of lemon juice, optional

A lovely, refreshing, summery pesto, perfect with a delicate egg pasta, such as fettuccine. Fresh green peas are best if you can get them, otherwise use tender young frozen peas – petits pois.

1 First fill a large saucepan with 4 quarts of water and bring to a boil over high heat for the pasta.

2 Meanwhile, make the pesto – or this can be done well in advance if you prefer. Follow the recipe on page 76, using mint instead of basil and leaving out the Parmesan cheese.

3 When the water in the saucepan boils, add the pasta along with a tablespoon of salt and give the pasta a quick stir. Briefly put the lid on until it starts to lift, showing that the water has come back to a boil, then let the pasta bubble away, uncovered, for about 8 minutes, or until it is tender but still has some bite to it.

4 While the fettuccine is cooking, bring ½ inch of water to a boil for the peas. Cook them for 2–3 minutes, then drain.

5 Reserve about a cup of water from the pasta. Drain the pasta by tipping it all into a colander placed in the sink, then put it back into the still-warm pan. Give the pesto a stir and loosen it a bit, if it needs it, by mixing in a couple of tablespoons of the hot pasta water, then add it to the pasta, along with the peas. Toss the pasta gently until it is all coated with the pesto, check the seasoning, then serve at once on warm plates.

FUSILLI LUNGHI WITH CRUNCHY NUT PESTO Serves ❹

INGREDIENTS

14 ounces fusilli lunghi

salt

fresh parsley, preferably flat-leaf, to serve

FOR THE PESTO:

½ cup walnuts, pecans or cashews, toasted

2 Tbs pine nuts, toasted (see page 78)

2 garlic cloves, peeled

1 Tbs soy sauce

¼ cup olive oil

salt and freshly ground black pepper

squeeze of lemon juice, optional

Pesto made with extra nuts is crunchy, delicious and best, I think, with a fairly substantial pasta.

1 First fill a large saucepan with 4 quarts of water and bring to a boil over high heat for the pasta.

2 Meanwhile, make the pesto – or this can be done well in advance if you prefer. Follow the recipe on page 76, leaving out the Parmesan and using the nuts instead of the basil, only ¼ cup of oil, a tablespoon of soy sauce and 3 tablespoons of water.

3 When the water in the saucepan boils, add the pasta along with a tablespoon of salt and give the pasta a quick stir. Briefly put the lid on until it starts to lift, showing that the water has come back to a boil, then let the pasta bubble away, uncovered, for about 8 minutes, or until it is tender but still has some bite to it.

4 Reserve about a cup of water from the pasta. Drain the pasta by tipping it all into a colander placed in the sink, then put it back into the still-warm pan. Stir the pesto and loosen it a bit, if it needs it, by mixing in a couple of tablespoons of the hot pasta water, then add it to the pasta. Toss the pasta gently until it is all coated with the pesto, check the seasoning, then serve at once on warm plates. Tear or snip the parsley over the top.

CREAM SAUCE Serves ❹

INGREDIENTS

2 Tbs butter

1 onion, peeled and chopped

2 garlic cloves, peeled and crushed

1¼ cups cream — light, heavy or soy cream

salt and freshly ground black pepper

freshly grated nutmeg

This rich sauce is wonderful for a special meal. It can be made with heavy cream for the most classic and, of course, luscious result, but both light dairy cream and the soy creams that are now available also give very good results.

1 Melt the butter in a small saucepan, then add the onion. Cover and cook gently for 10 minutes, until tender but not brown.

2 Add garlic to the onion and cook for a minute or two longer. Stir in the cream and leave the mixture to simmer gently for about 10 minutes, until the cream has reduced a bit and thickened.

3 Season with salt, pepper and nutmeg and keep on one side until the pasta is done.

TAGLIATELLE WITH GORGONZOLA CREAM SAUCE Serves ❹

INGREDIENTS

14 ounces tagliatelle

salt

1 quantity of cream sauce (above)

4 ounces Gorgonzola cheese, diced

1 Tbs olive oil, optional

freshly ground black pepper

This is rich and wonderful. You could use another type of blue cheese if you prefer, and, as for the cream sauce, the light-cream version is best since the cheese adds so much richness.

1 First fill a large saucepan with 4 quarts of water and bring to a boil over high heat for the pasta.

2 When the water boils, add the pasta along with a tablespoon of salt and give the pasta a quick stir. Briefly put the lid on until it starts to lift, showing that the water has come back to a boil, then let the pasta bubble away, uncovered, for about 8 minutes, or until it is tender but still has some bite to it.

3 Heat the cream sauce through gently. Just before the pasta is ready, remove the sauce from the heat and add the Gorgonzola, so that it begins to melt.

4 Drain the pasta by tipping it all into a colander placed in the sink, then put it back into the still-warm pan. Either add the olive oil to the pasta, serve it on warm plates and spoon the sauce on top; or add the sauce directly to the pasta, toss gently and serve on warm plates. Grind some black pepper coarsely over the top and serve at once.

FUSILLI IN CREAM SAUCE WITH ASPARAGUS AND SUMMER HERBS Serves ❹

INGREDIENTS

1 pound asparagus, trimmed and cut into 1-inch lengths

14 ounces fusilli

salt

1 quantity of cream sauce (opposite)

freshly ground black pepper

squeeze of lemon juice, optional

1 Tbs olive oil

2 Tbs chopped or torn fresh flat-leaf parsley, chervil and chives, to serve

A wonderful summer pasta dish; serve it with a delicate, leafy salad and chilled white wine.

1 First fill a large saucepan with 4 quarts of water and bring to a boil over high heat for the pasta.

2 Meanwhile, cook the asparagus in a little boiling water for 6–8 minutes, or until tender. Drain the asparagus and keep it warm.

3 When the water in the saucepan boils, add the pasta along with a tablespoon of salt and give the pasta a quick stir. Briefly put the lid on until it starts to lift, showing that the water has come back to a boil, then let the pasta bubble away, uncovered, for about 8 minutes, or until it is tender but still has some bite to it.

4 Heat the cream sauce through gently. Add the asparagus and check the seasoning, adding pepper, a squeeze of lemon juice and salt to taste if it needs it.

5 Drain the pasta by tipping it all into a colander placed in the sink, then put it back into the still-warm pan. Either add the olive oil to the pasta, serve it on warm plates and spoon the sauce on top; or add the sauce directly to the pasta, toss gently and serve on warm plates. Scatter the herbs on top and serve at once.

PAPPARDELLE IN CREAM SAUCE WITH PORCINI Serves ❹

INGREDIENTS

14 ounces pappardelle

salt

2 Tbs butter

4 cups fresh porcini
mushrooms, cleaned and sliced

1 garlic clove, peeled and crushed

1 quantity of cream sauce (page 82)

squeeze of lemon juice, optional

freshly ground black pepper

1 Tbs olive oil, optional

sprigs of fresh flat-leaf parsley,
to serve

If you are lucky enough to be able to get some, fresh porcini (also called ceps) are a wonderful treat.

1 First fill a large saucepan with 4 quarts of water and bring to a boil over high heat for the pasta.

2 When the water boils, add the pasta along with a tablespoon of salt and give the pasta a quick stir. Briefly put the lid on until it starts to lift, showing that the water has come back to a boil, then let the pasta bubble away, uncovered, for about 8 minutes, or until it is tender but still has some bite to it.

3 Meanwhile, cook the porcini mushrooms. Melt the butter in a medium saucepan, add the mushrooms and garlic and cook for 4–5 minutes, or until the mushrooms are

tender and any liquid has disappeared, stirring from time to time. Keep the porcini mushrooms warm.

4 Heat the cream sauce through gently. Check the seasoning, adding a squeeze of lemon juice if it needs it.

5 Drain the pasta by tipping it all into a colander placed in the sink, then put it back into the still-warm pan. Either add the olive oil to the pasta, serve it on warm plates and spoon the sauce on top; or add the sauce directly to the pasta, toss gently and serve on warm plates. Spoon the porcini on top, tear or snip the parsley over, and serve at once.

TAGLIATELLE IN CREAM SAUCE WITH GRUYÈRE, PARMESAN AND FLAT-LEAF PARSLEY Serves ❹

INGREDIENTS

14 ounces tagliatelle

salt

1 quantity of cream sauce (page 82)

1 cup grated Gruyère cheese

⅔ cup freshly grated
Parmesan cheese

1 Tbs olive oil, optional

freshly ground black pepper

sprigs of fresh parsley, preferably
flat-leaf, to serve

As this is rich with added cheeses, I find the light-cream version of the cream sauce is best. It is for when you feel like a soothing, indulgent dish.

1 First fill a large saucepan with 4 quarts of water and bring to a boil over high heat for the pasta.

2 When the water boils, add the pasta along with a tablespoon of salt and give the pasta a quick stir. Briefly put the lid on until it starts to lift, showing that the water has come back to a boil, then let the pasta bubble away, uncovered, for about 8 minutes, or until it is tender but still has some bite to it.

3 Heat the cream sauce through gently. Just before the pasta is done, add all the Gruyère and half of the Parmesan cheese to the sauce.

4 Drain the pasta by tipping it all into a colander placed in the sink, then put it back into the still-warm pan. Either add the olive oil to the pasta, serve it on warm plates and spoon the sauce on top; or add the sauce directly to the pasta in the pan, toss gently and serve on warm plates. Coarsely grind some black pepper to taste over the pasta, scatter with the remaining Parmesan cheese and tear the sprigs of parsley over the top. Serve at once.

Pappardelle in cream
sauce with porcini

FETTUCCINE IN CREAM SAUCE WITH FRESH PEAS AND MINT Serves ❹

This is wonderful made with tender fresh peas, but also very good with frozen petits pois.

1 First fill a large saucepan with 4 quarts of water and bring to a boil over high heat for the pasta.

2 When the water boils, add the pasta along with a tablespoon of salt and give the pasta a quick stir. Briefly put the lid on until it starts to lift, showing that the water has come back to a boil, then let the pasta bubble away, uncovered, for about 8 minutes, or until it is tender but still has some bite to it.

3 Add the peas to the cream sauce in a pan and cook over a gentle heat, to heat through both the peas and the sauce. Check the seasoning, adding a little salt and pepper to taste if it needs it.

4 Drain the pasta by tipping it all into a colander placed in the sink, then put it back into the still-warm pan. Either add the olive oil to the pasta, serve it on warm plates and spoon the sauce on top; or add the sauce directly to the pasta, toss gently and serve on warm plates. Scatter the chopped mint on top and serve at once.

FETTUCCINE WITH DOLCELATTE CREAM SAUCE AND SPINACH Serves ❹

If you cannot get dolcelatte, use any other type of blue cheese for this delicious dish.

1 First fill a large saucepan with 4 quarts of water and bring to a boil over high heat for the pasta.

2 When the water boils, add the pasta along with a tablespoon of salt and give the pasta a quick stir. Briefly put the lid on until it starts to lift, showing that the water has come back to a boil, then let the pasta bubble away, uncovered, for about 8 minutes, or until it is tender but still has some bite to it.

3 Heat the cream sauce through gently. Just before the pasta is ready, add the dolcelatte and spinach to the sauce and stir for 1–2 minutes over the heat. Season with some pepper – it probably will not need any salt because the cheese will have added some.

4 Drain the pasta by tipping it all into a colander placed in the sink, then put it back into the still-warm pan. Either add the olive oil to the pasta, serve it on warm plates and spoon the sauce on top; or add the sauce directly to the pasta, toss gently and serve on warm plates.

TAGLIATELLE VERDE IN CREAM SAUCE WITH OYSTER MUSHROOMS AND GARLIC Serves ❹

INGREDIENTS

14 ounces tagliatelle verde

salt

2 Tbs butter

4 cups oyster mushrooms, cleaned and sliced

1 garlic clove, peeled and crushed

1 quantity of cream sauce (page 82)

freshly ground black pepper

squeeze of lemon juice, optional

1 Tbs olive oil

sprigs of fresh flat-leaf parsley, to serve

Oyster mushrooms, with their delicate flavor and texture, are excellent in this dish.

1 First fill a large saucepan with 4 quarts of water and bring to a boil over high heat for the pasta.

2 When the water boils, add the pasta along with a tablespoon of salt and give the pasta a quick stir. Briefly put the lid on until it starts to lift, showing that the water has come back to a boil, then let the pasta bubble away, uncovered, for about 8 minutes, or until it is tender but still has some bite to it.

3 Meanwhile, cook the oyster mushrooms: melt the butter in a medium saucepan, add the mushrooms and garlic and cook for 4–5 minutes, or until they are tender and any liquid has disappeared, stirring from time to time to cook evenly.

4 Heat the cream sauce through gently. Add the mushrooms and check the seasoning, adding pepper, a squeeze of lemon juice and salt to taste if it needs it.

5 Drain the pasta by tipping it all into a colander placed in the sink, then put it back into the still-warm pan. Either add the olive oil to the pasta, serve it on warm plates and spoon the sauce on top; or add the sauce directly to the pasta, toss gently and serve on warm plates. Chop, snip or tear the parsley over the top.

PENNE WITH CHILI-CREAM SAUCE Serves ❹

INGREDIENTS

14 ounces penne

salt

1 dried red chili, crumbled

1 Tbs sun-dried tomato paste

1 quantity of cream sauce (page 82)

freshly ground black pepper

1 Tbs olive oil, optional

fresh basil leaves, to serve

The chili takes the richness away from the sauce and gives it an unexpected and pleasant note.

1 First fill a large saucepan with 4 quarts of water and bring to a boil over high heat for the pasta.

2 When the water boils, add the pasta along with a tablespoon of salt and give the pasta a quick stir. Briefly put the lid on until it starts to lift, showing that the water has come back to a boil, then let the pasta bubble away, uncovered, for about 8 minutes, or until it is tender but still has some bite to it.

3 Stir the chili and sun-dried tomato paste into the cream sauce in a pan and heat through gently. Check the seasoning, adding salt and pepper to taste if it needs it.

4 Drain the pasta by tipping it all into a colander placed in the sink, then put it back into the still-warm pan. Either add the olive oil to the pasta, serve it on warm plates and spoon the sauce on top; or add the sauce directly to the pasta, toss gently and serve on warm plates. Tear the basil leaves over the top and serve at once.

FUSILLI IN CREAM SAUCE WITH YOUNG SUMMER VEGETABLES Serves ❹

INGREDIENTS

4 ounces baby new carrots, trimmed and scrubbed

8 ounces asparagus, trimmed and cut into ½-inch lengths

14 ounces fusilli

salt

1⅓ cups shelled fresh fava beans

1 quantity of cream sauce (page 82)

¼ cup shelled fresh peas

freshly ground black pepper

squeeze of lemon juice, optional

1 Tbs olive oil, optional

sprigs of fresh chervil, to serve

Another summery dish, although you could make it at any time of the year when you feel like a taste of sunshine.

1 First fill a large saucepan with 4 quarts of water and bring to a boil over high heat for the pasta.

2 Meanwhile, cook the baby carrots and asparagus in a little boiling water for 6–8 minutes, or until they are tender; drain the vegetables and keep them warm.

3 When the water in the saucepan boils, add the pasta along with a tablespoon of salt and give the pasta a quick stir. Briefly put the lid on until it starts to lift, showing that the water has come back to a boil, then let the pasta bubble away, uncovered, for about 8 minutes, or until it is tender but still has some bite to it.

4 Meanwhile, cook the fava beans in boiling water for 1 minute; drain, refresh under cold water, then pop the beans out of their skins.

5 Add the fava beans to the cream sauce in a pan, along with the peas, and heat through gently. Just before the pasta is ready, add the carrots and asparagus. Check the seasoning, adding pepper and a squeeze of lemon juice to taste if it needs it.

6 Drain the pasta by tipping it all into a colander placed in the sink, then put it back into the still-warm pan. Either add the olive oil to the pasta, serve it on warm plates and spoon the vegetable sauce on top; or add the vegetable sauce directly to the pasta, toss gently and serve on warm plates. Scatter some sprigs of the fresh chervil on top and serve at once.

BÉCHAMEL SAUCE Serves ❹

INGREDIENTS

4 Tbs butter

6 Tbs flour

2½ cups milk

I bay leaf

a few stalks of parsley if available

slice of onion if available

a little extra milk — see method

¼–½ cup cream, optional

salt and freshly ground black pepper

freshly grated nutmeg

Classic béchamel sauce is comforting and makes a good base for variations. If you want to reduce the calories, use skim milk (or soy milk) and omit the cream, or try the completely nonclassic but useful low-fat béchamel sauce that follows.

1 Melt the butter in a saucepan and stir in the flour. When it froths, stir in half the milk and beat well over the heat until it thickens. Add the rest of the milk and keep stirring vigorously, still over the heat, until the sauce is thick and smooth.

2 Add the bay leaf, parsley stalks and slice of onion if using, then leave the sauce over a very low heat for 10 minutes. Thin the sauce by stirring in a little extra milk if necessary. If you are making the sauce well in advance, do not stir in this extra milk but pour it over the top of the sauce and leave it, to prevent a skin from forming.

3 When you are ready to use the sauce, give it a stir, remove the bay leaf, parsley and onion, add the cream if using and season with salt, pepper and nutmeg.

•

Mix béchamel in a blender if it is lumpy – this also seems to make the sauce taste creamier, so I often do it anyway.

LOW-FAT BÉCHAMEL SAUCE Serves ❹

INGREDIENTS

5 Tbs cornstarch

2½ cups low-fat milk
or unsweetened soy milk

I bay leaf

a few stalks of parsley if available

slice of onion if available

I Tbs Dijon mustard

salt and freshly ground black pepper

freshly grated nutmeg

a little extra milk, optional —
see method

This is a very useful sauce for anyone who is counting calories. It is surprisingly flavorful and makes an excellent base for adding other interesting ingredients. You can substitute this for ordinary béchamel in any of the recipes.

1 Put the cornstarch into a bowl and mix to a thin paste with a little of the milk. Bring the rest of the milk to a boil with the bay leaf, and the parsley and slice of onion if using.

2 Pour a boiling milk over the cornstarch mixture, stirring well, then pour the mixture back into the pan. Stir over a moderate heat for a couple of minutes until the mixture has thickened, then remove from the heat. Stir in the mustard and season with salt, pepper and nutmeg.

3 If you are making the sauce well in advance, pour a little milk over the surface of the sauce and leave it to prevent a skin from forming.

4 When you are ready to use the sauce, remove the bay leaf, onion and parsley. Give the sauce a stir and check the seasoning, adding salt, pepper and nutmeg to taste if it needs it.

LUMACHE WITH BROCCOLI BÉCHAMEL Serves ❹

INGREDIENTS

14 ounces lumache

salt

4 cups trimmed broccoli florets, roughly chopped

1 quantity of béchamel sauce or low-fat béchamel sauce (opposite)

freshly ground black pepper

freshly grated nutmeg

squeeze of lemon juice, optional

1 Tbs olive oil, optional

Broccoli and béchamel is a winning combination. I like to serve this pasta dish with a tomato salad – perhaps little cherry tomatoes, halved and tossed in a light vinaigrette – and some warm bread for those who want it. Other short pastas could be used: gnocchi or conchiglie, for instance.

1 First fill a large saucepan with 4 quarts of water and bring to a boil over high heat for the pasta.

2 When the water boils, add the pasta along with a tablespoon of salt and give the pasta a quick stir. Briefly put the lid on until it starts to lift, showing that the water has come back to a boil, then let the pasta bubble away, uncovered, for about 8 minutes, or until it is tender but still has some bite to it.

3 Meanwhile, cook the broccoli in a little boiling water for 3–4 minutes, or until it is just tender, then drain and add to the béchamel sauce.

4 Heat the béchamel sauce through gently and check the seasoning, adding pepper, nutmeg, a squeeze of lemon juice and more salt to taste if it needs it.

5 Drain the pasta by tipping it all into a colander placed in the sink, then put it back into the still-warm pan. Either add the olive oil to the pasta, serve it on warm plates and spoon the sauce on top; or add the sauce directly to the pasta, toss gently and serve on warm plates.

SPAGHETTI WITH BÉCHAMEL SAUCE, PESTO AND PARMESAN Serves ❹

INGREDIENTS

14 ounces spaghetti

salt

1 quantity of béchamel sauce or low-fat béchamel sauce (opposite)

4 Tbs basil pesto sauce, store-bought or homemade (page 76)

freshly ground black pepper

1 Tbs olive oil, optional

⅔–1⅓ cups fresh Parmesan cheese, cut in flakes or grated

fresh parsley or basil leaves, to serve

You could use homemade pesto (page 76) for this, or one of the good bottled ones that are now available.

1 First fill a large saucepan with 4 quarts of water and bring to a boil over high heat for the pasta.

2 When the water boils, add the spaghetti, holding it straight up like a bunch of flowers and gently pushing it into the water as it softens. Add a tablespoon of salt and give the pasta a quick stir. Briefly put the lid on until it starts to lift, showing that the water has come back to a boil, then let the pasta bubble away, uncovered, for about 8 minutes, or until it is tender but still has some bite to it.

3 Meanwhile, heat the béchamel sauce through gently. Stir in the pesto and check the seasoning, adding salt and pepper as necessary.

4 Drain the spaghetti by tipping it all into a colander placed in the sink, then put it back into the still-warm pan. Either add the olive oil to the pasta, serve it on warm plates and spoon the sauce on top; or add the sauce directly to the pasta, toss gently and serve on warm plates. Scatter generously with the Parmesan and tear or snip the parsley or basil over the top.

TAGLIATELLE IN MUSHROOM AND GARLIC BÉCHAMEL SAUCE WITH PARSLEY Serves ❹

INGREDIENTS

14 ounces tagliatelle

salt

2 Tbs butter

4 cups mushrooms, cleaned and sliced

2 garlic cloves, peeled and crushed

1 quantity of béchamel sauce or low-fat béchamel sauce (page 90)

freshly ground black pepper

squeeze of lemon juice, optional

1 Tbs olive oil, optional

bunch of fresh flat-leaf parsley and freshly grated Parmesan cheese, to serve

This is good made with tagliatelle, but the short pastas are also suitable, particularly a chunky one, such as gnocchi or lumache.

1 First fill a large saucepan with 4 quarts of water and bring to a boil over high heat for the pasta.

2 When the water boils, add the pasta along with a tablespoon of salt and give the pasta a quick stir. Briefly put the lid on until it starts to lift, showing that the water has come back to a boil, then let the pasta bubble away, uncovered, for about 8 minutes, or until it is tender but still has some bite to it.

3 Meanwhile, cook the mushrooms: melt the butter in a medium saucepan, add the mushrooms and garlic and cook for 4–5 minutes, or until tender and any liquid has disappeared, stirring from time to time.

4 Heat the béchamel sauce through gently, stir in the mushrooms and check the seasoning, adding pepper, a squeeze of lemon juice and salt to taste if it needs it.

5 Drain the tagliatelle by tipping it all into a colander placed in the sink, then put it back into the still-warm pan. Either add the olive oil to the pasta, serve it on warm plates and spoon the sauce on top; or add the sauce directly to the pasta, toss gently and serve on warm plates. Tear or snip plenty of parsley over the top, and hand around freshly grated Parmesan.

CONCHIGLIE WITH BÉCHAMEL SAUCE, FRESH HERBS AND PINE NUTS Serves ❹

INGREDIENTS

14 ounces conchiglie

salt

1 quantity of béchamel sauce or low-fat béchamel sauce (page 90)

5–6 Tbs chopped fresh herbs: parsley, chives and chervil if available

freshly ground black pepper

squeeze of lemon juice, optional

½ cup pine nuts, toasted (see page 78)

1 Tbs olive oil, optional

sprigs of fresh parsley and flakes of Parmesan cheese, to serve

This is simple but very good: the fresh herbs really make it, and the pine nuts give a pleasant crunch, as well as adding flavor.

1 First fill a large saucepan with 4 quarts of water and bring to a boil over high heat for the pasta.

2 When the water boils, add the pasta along with a tablespoon of salt and give the pasta a quick stir. Briefly put the lid on until it starts to lift, showing that the water has come back to a boil, then let the pasta bubble away, uncovered, for about 8 minutes, or until it is tender but still has some bite to it.

3 Meanwhile, heat the béchamel sauce through gently, then stir in the herbs and check the seasoning, adding some grindings of pepper and a squeeze of lemon juice to taste if it needs it.

4 Drain the pasta by tipping it all into a colander placed in the sink, then put it back into the still-warm pan with the pine nuts. Either add the olive oil to the pasta, serve it on warm plates and spoon the sauce on top; or add the sauce directly to the pasta, toss gently and serve on warm plates. Decorate with sprigs of parsley or chervil and scatter Parmesan over the top.

FUSILLI AND CORN IN BÉCHAMEL SAUCE WITH RED AND GREEN BELL PEPPERS Serves ❹

INGREDIENTS

14 ounces fusilli

salt

1¼ cups fresh corn scraped from the cob or frozen or canned corn

1 quantity of béchamel sauce or low-fat béchamel sauce (page 90)

1 small red bell pepper, de-seeded and finely chopped

1 small green bell pepper, de-seeded and finely chopped

freshly ground black pepper

squeeze of lemon juice, optional

1 Tbs olive oil, optional

I have found this dish to be popular with children, all of whom seem to like corn and enjoy the bright colors of the peppers. Use their favorite pasta shape: butterflies (farfalle), shells (conchiglie) or snails (lumache) are as good as spirals (fusilli).

1 First fill a large saucepan with 4 quarts of water and bring to a boil over high heat for the pasta.

2 When the water boils, add the pasta along with a tablespoon of salt and give the pasta a quick stir. Briefly put the lid on until it starts to lift, showing that the water has come back to a boil, then let the pasta bubble away, uncovered, for about 8 minutes, or until it is tender but still has some bite to it.

3 Meanwhile, cook the corn in a little boiling water for 3–4 minutes, or until it is just tender, then drain and add to the béchamel sauce along with the chopped bell peppers.

4 Heat the béchamel sauce through gently, then check the seasoning, adding pepper, a squeeze of lemon juice and salt to taste if it needs it.

5 Drain the pasta by tipping it all into a colander placed in the sink, then put it back into the still-warm pan. Either add the olive oil to the pasta, serve it on warm plates and spoon the sauce on top; or add the sauce directly to the pasta, toss gently and serve on warm plates.

SPINACH TAGLIATELLE WITH BÉCHAMEL SAUCE AND THREE CHEESES Serves ❹

INGREDIENTS

14 ounces spinach tagliatelle (tagliatelle verde)

salt

2 4-ounce firm goat cheese logs, each sliced into 4 rounds

1 quantity of béchamel sauce or low-fat béchamel sauce (page 90)

⅔ cup freshly grated Parmesan cheese

freshly ground black pepper

1 Tbs olive oil

4 ounces blue cheese, crumbled

sprigs of flat-leaf parsley, to serve

You could use a different selection of cheeses than those given here, but choose three contrasting ones so that the flavors are distinct because they soften and melt in the hot sauce.

1 First fill a large saucepan with 4 quarts of water and bring to a boil over high heat for the pasta.

2 When the water boils, add the pasta along with a tablespoon of salt and give the pasta a quick stir. Briefly put the lid on until it starts to lift, showing that the water has come back to a boil, then let the pasta bubble away, uncovered, for about 8 minutes, or until it is tender but still has some bite to it.

3 Just before the pasta is done, set the broiler to high. Line the broiler pan with foil and place the rounds of goat cheese on it; broil for 3–4 minutes until they are golden brown and beginning to melt.

4 Heat the béchamel sauce through gently. Stir in half the Parmesan cheese and check the seasoning, adding salt and pepper as necessary.

5 Drain the pasta by tipping it all into a colander placed in the sink, then put it back into the still-warm pan. Add the olive oil and toss gently. Serve the pasta on warmed plates, spoon the sauce on top, then scatter with the crumbled blue cheese and remaining Parmesan and place two rounds of goat cheese on each serving. Garnish with a few sprigs of flat-leaf parsley.

FARFALLE WITH BÉCHAMEL SAUCE, BROILED FENNEL AND PINE NUTS Serves ❹

INGREDIENTS

I pound fennel bulbs, trimmed, reserving any feathery leaves, and sliced into eighths

olive oil

14 ounces farfalle

salt

I quantity of béchamel sauce or low-fat béchamel sauce (page 90)

freshly ground black pepper

squeeze of lemon juice, optional

½ cup pine nuts, toasted (see page 78)

Broiled fennel is easy to do and a delicious ingredient in this pasta dish. If you do not like fennel, or cannot get it, use broiled pepper strips instead. The dish would be rather different, but also very good.

1 First fill a large saucepan with 4 quarts of water and bring to a boil over high heat for the pasta.

2 Meanwhile, par-boil the fennel in a little boiling water for 4–5 minutes until just tender. Then drain well, brush lightly all over with olive oil, put in a single layer on a broiler pan or cookie sheet that will fit under your broiler, and broil under high heat until tender and tinged with brown: 4–5 minutes. Keep the fennel warm.

3 When the water in the saucepan boils, add the pasta along with a tablespoon of salt and give the pasta a quick stir. Briefly put the lid on until it starts to lift, showing that the water has come back to a boil, then let the pasta bubble away, uncovered, for about 8 minutes, or until it is tender but still has some bite to it.

4 Heat the béchamel sauce through gently. Chop any reserved fennel leaves and add to the sauce. Check the seasoning, adding a squeeze of lemon juice if it needs it.

5 Drain the pasta by tipping it all into a colander placed in the sink, then put it back into the still-warm pan. Either add 1 tablespoon of olive oil to the pasta, serve it on warm plates and spoon the sauce on top; or add the sauce directly to the pasta, toss gently and serve on warm plates. In either case, top each portion with slices of broiled fennel and pine nuts and serve at once.

FARFALLE BÉCHAMEL WITH LEEKS, OLIVES AND SUN-DRIED TOMATOES Serves ❹

INGREDIENTS

1 pound leeks, trimmed and cut into ¼ inch slices

8 sun-dried tomatoes, drained of oil and roughly chopped

⅔ cup black olives

14 ounces farfalle

salt

1 quantity of béchamel sauce or low-fat béchamel sauce (page 90)

freshly ground black pepper

squeeze of lemon juice, optional

1 Tbs olive oil, optional

fresh flat-leaf parsley and flakes of Parmesan cheese, to serve

This is a wonderfully tasty, filling mixture. It really doesn't need any accompaniment except perhaps some warm bread – a whole wheat walnut loaf – if you are very hungry.

1 First fill a large saucepan with 4 quarts of water and bring to a boil over high heat for the pasta.

2 Meanwhile, cook the leeks in a little boiling water for about 6 minutes, until tender. Drain the leeks, return them to the pan and add the sun-dried tomatoes and olives.

3 When the water in the saucepan boils, add the pasta along with a tablespoon of salt and give the pasta a quick stir. Briefly put the lid on until it starts to lift, showing that the water has come back to a boil, then let the pasta bubble away, uncovered, for about 8 minutes, or until it is tender but still has some bite to it.

4 Heat the béchamel sauce through gently and add half the leek mixture. Check the seasoning, adding a squeeze of lemon juice if it needs it.

5 Drain the pasta by tipping it all into a colander placed in the sink, then put it back into the still-warm pan. Either add the olive oil to the pasta, serve it on warm plates and spoon the sauce on top; or add the sauce directly to the pasta, toss gently and serve on warm plates. Top with the remaining leek mixture, tear or snip a little parsley over, scatter with the Parmesan and serve at once.

FETTUCCINE BÉCHAMEL WITH BROILED ASPARAGUS, LEMON AND PARSLEY Serves ❹

INGREDIENTS

14 ounces fettuccine

salt

1 pound asparagus, trimmed and halved to make pieces approx. 2 inches long

olive oil

1 quantity of béchamel sauce or low-fat béchamel sauce (page 90)

freshly ground black pepper

squeeze of lemon juice, optional

finely shredded rind of 1 lemon and flakes of Parmesan cheese, to serve

Broiling is a very good way to cook asparagus; it is easier than boiling or steaming it, and the result is excellent. If you want to save a few calories, though, better boil or steam it.

1 First fill a large saucepan with 4 quarts of water and bring to a boil over high heat for the pasta.

2 When the water boils, add the pasta along with a tablespoon of salt and give the pasta a quick stir. Briefly put the lid on until it starts to lift, showing that the water has come back to a boil, then let the pasta bubble away, uncovered, for about 8 minutes, or until it is tender but still has some bite to it.

3 Meanwhile, brush the asparagus with a little olive oil and broil under high heat until tender and lightly browned: 6–8 minutes, turning the asparagus over halfway through.

4 Heat the béchamel sauce through gently. Check the seasoning, adding pepper and a squeeze of lemon juice to taste if it needs it.

5 Drain the pasta by tipping it all into a colander placed in the sink, then put it back into the still-warm pan. Either add 1 tablespoon of olive oil to the pasta, serve it on warm plates and spoon the sauce on top; or add the sauce directly to the pasta, toss gently and serve on warm plates. Top with the asparagus and lemon zest (rind). Scatter with Parmesan, grind black pepper over and serve at once.

•

A citrus zester is quite cheap to buy and very useful. Grasp the lemon, or other citrus fruit, and run the zester firmly down its skin to produce long slim ribbons of zest with no pith attached. If you do not have a zester, pare off thin slices of skin with a potato peeler, then cut into thin shreds.

LENTIL BOLOGNESE SAUCE Serves ❹

INGREDIENTS

⅔ cup whole green or brown lentils or split orange lentils, or 14 ounces canned green lentils

1 onion, peeled and chopped

2 Tbs olive oil

2 garlic cloves, peeled and crushed

1 celery stalk, chopped

1 carrot, finely diced

2 tomatoes, skinned and chopped

1 tsp sun-dried tomato paste

1 Tbs chopped parsley

salt and freshly ground black pepper

Lentils – indeed, any legumes – make a great combination with pasta: protein-packed and filling. A lentil sauce makes a good vegetarian version of a bolognese sauce and lots of variations are possible. You can use either whole lentils or the split orange ones – each gives a different result, and both are good.

1 If you are using any type of dried lentils, put them into a saucepan with 2¼ cups of water and bring to a boil, then let them simmer gently until they are tender: 40 minutes or so for the brown or green lentils, about 20 minutes for the orange ones. Drain the lentils, whether freshly cooked or canned, keeping the liquid.

2 Sauté the onion in the oil for 5 minutes, then add the garlic, celery and carrots. Cover and leave to cook gently for 15 minutes until tender, stirring from time to time.

3 Add the lentils, tomatoes, sun-dried tomato paste and enough of the reserved liquid to make a thick, soft consistency. Simmer for about 10 minutes, adding more liquid if necessary. Stir in the chopped parsley and season to taste with salt and freshly ground black pepper.

SPAGHETTI WITH LENTIL BOLOGNESE SAUCE AND SUN-DRIED TOMATOES Serves ❹

INGREDIENTS

14 ounces spaghetti

salt

8 sun-dried tomatoes, drained of oil and roughly chopped

1 quantity of lentil bolognese sauce (above)

freshly ground black pepper

1 Tbs olive oil, optional

sprigs of fresh parsley or chervil, to serve

fresh Parmesan cheese, cut in flakes or grated, to serve

The sun-dried tomatoes add a lovely richness to this sauce. It is good with both spaghetti and tagliatelle.

1 First fill a large saucepan with 4 quarts of water and bring to a boil over high heat for the pasta.

2 When the water boils, add the spaghetti, holding it straight up like a bunch of flowers and gently pushing it into the water as it softens. Add a tablespoon of salt and give the pasta a quick stir. Briefly put the lid on until it starts to lift, showing that the water has come back to a boil, then let the pasta bubble away, uncovered, for about 8 minutes, or until it is tender but still has some bite to it.

3 Meanwhile, stir the chopped sun-dried tomatoes into the bolognese sauce in a pan and heat through gently. Check the seasoning, adding salt and pepper to taste if it needs it.

4 Drain the pasta by tipping it all into a colander placed in the sink, then put it back into the still-warm pan. Either add the olive oil to the pasta, serve it on warm plates and spoon the sauce on top; or add the sauce directly to the pasta, toss gently and serve on warm plates. Tear the parsley or chervil over the top, scatter with Parmesan flakes and serve at once.

TAGLIATELLE WITH LENTIL AND WINE SAUCE Serves ❹

INGREDIENTS

14 ounces tagliatelle

salt

glass of red wine

1 quantity of lentil bolognese sauce (opposite)

freshly ground black pepper

1 Tbs olive oil, optional

fresh basil leaves and flakes of Parmesan cheese, to serve

This is rich-tasting and warming; great to come back to on a chilly winter's night.

1 First fill a large saucepan with 4 quarts of water and bring to a boil over high heat for the pasta.

2 When the water boils, add the pasta along with a tablespoon of salt and give the pasta a quick stir. Briefly put the lid on until it starts to lift, showing that the water has come back to a boil, then let the pasta bubble away, uncovered, for about 8 minutes, or until it is tender but still has some bite to it.

3 Meanwhile, add the wine to the bolognese sauce in a pan, bring to a boil, then let simmer gently. Check the seasoning, adding salt and pepper to taste if it needs it.

4 Drain the pasta by tipping it all into a colander placed in the sink, then put it back into the still-warm pan. Either add the olive oil to the pasta, serve it on warm plates and spoon the sauce on top; or add the sauce directly to the pasta, toss gently and serve on warm plates. Tear basil leaves over the top, scatter with flakes of Parmesan and serve at once.

FUSILLI LUNGHI WITH MUSHROOMS IN LENTIL BOLOGNESE SAUCE Serves ❹

INGREDIENTS

14 ounces fusilli lunghi

salt

2 cups mushrooms, cleaned and sliced

olive oil

2 garlic cloves, peeled and crushed

1 quantity of lentil bolognese sauce (opposite)

freshly ground black pepper

fresh Parmesan cheese, cut in flakes or grated, to serve

1 First fill a large saucepan with 4 quarts of water and bring to a boil over high heat for the pasta.

2 When the water boils, add the pasta along with a tablespoon of salt and give the pasta a quick stir. Briefly put the lid on until it starts to lift, showing that the water has come back to a boil, then let the pasta bubble away, uncovered, for about 8 minutes, or until it is tender but still has some bite to it.

3 Sauté the mushrooms in 1 tablespoon of olive oil, with the garlic, for 4–5 minutes, until tender and any liquid has boiled away.

4 Add the mushrooms to the bolognese sauce in a pan and heat through gently. Check the seasoning, adding salt and pepper to taste if it needs it.

5 Drain the pasta by tipping it all into a colander placed in the sink, then put it back into the still-warm pan. Either add 1 tablespoon of olive oil to the pasta, serve it on warm plates and spoon the sauce on top; or add the sauce directly to the pasta, toss gently and serve on warm plates. Serve at once and hand around the Parmesan.

PENNE RIGATE WITH GOLDEN LENTIL BOLOGNESE SAUCE, RED BELL PEPPER AND LEEKS Serves ❹

INGREDIENTS

2 red bell peppers

8 ounces leeks, trimmed and cut into ¼-inch slices

olive oil, optional

14 ounces penne rigate

salt

1 quantity of lentil bolognese sauce (page 100), made with split orange lentils

freshly ground black pepper

A flavorful combination of ingredients, this colorful pasta dish is quite filling and needs no accompaniment, except perhaps for a glass of red wine.

1 First prepare the bell peppers for the sauce by cutting them into quarters and placing them, skin-side (shiny side) up, on a broiler pan. Put under high heat for 10–15 minutes, until the skin has blistered and blackened. Cover the peppers with a plate and leave until cool enough to handle, then remove the skin, stem and seeds, and cut the flesh into slices.

2 Next fill a large saucepan with 4 quarts of water and bring to a boil over high heat for the pasta.

3 Meanwhile, cook the leeks, either by sautéing them in 1 tablespoon of olive oil or, for a less rich result, in a little boiling water. Either way they will take about 6 minutes. Drain the leeks if necessary and keep them warm.

4 When the water in the saucepan boils, add the pasta along with a tablespoon of salt and give the pasta a quick stir. Briefly put the lid on until it starts to lift, showing that the water has come back to a boil, then let the pasta bubble away, uncovered, for about 8 minutes, or until it is tender but still has some bite to it.

5 Heat the bolognese sauce through gently. Check the seasoning, adding salt and pepper to taste if it needs it.

6 Drain the pasta by tipping it all into a colander placed in the sink, then put it back into the still-warm pan. Either add the olive oil to the pasta, serve it on warm plates and spoon the sauce on top; or add the sauce directly to the pasta, toss gently and serve on warm plates. Put the peppers and leeks on top and serve at once.

SPAGHETTI WITH LENTIL BOLOGNESE, FRESH PEAS AND MINT Serves ❹

INGREDIENTS

14 ounces spaghetti

salt

1 quantity of lentil bolognese sauce (page 100)

1½ cups shelled fresh peas or frozen petit pois

freshly ground black pepper

1 Tbs olive oil, optional

2–3 Tbs chopped fresh mint

The peas and mint give a surprisingly light, summery feeling to this hearty pasta dish. A tomato salad goes well with it.

1 First fill a large saucepan with 4 quarts of water and bring to a boil over high heat for the pasta.

2 When the water boils, add the spaghetti, holding it straight up like a bunch of flowers and gently pushing it into the water as it softens. Add a tablespoon of salt and give the pasta a quick stir. Briefly put the lid on until it starts to lift, showing that the water has come back to a boil, then let the pasta bubble away, uncovered, for about 8 minutes, or until it is tender but still has some bite to it.

3 Meanwhile, gently reheat the bolognese sauce. Just before the pasta is done, add the peas to the sauce and cook gently for a minute or two, to heat the peas through. Check the seasoning, adding salt and pepper to taste if it needs it.

4 Drain the pasta by tipping it all into a colander placed in the sink, then put it back into the still-warm pan. Either add the olive oil to the pasta, serve it on warm plates and spoon the sauce on top; or add the sauce directly to the pasta, toss gently and serve on warm plates. Scatter the mint on top and serve at once.

LASAGNETTE WITH SPICED LENTIL AND TOMATO BOLOGNESE SAUCE Serves ❹

INGREDIENTS

1 cup canned tomatoes

½ tsp ground cinnamon

1 tsp chopped fresh oregano or ½ tsp dried oregano

1 quantity of lentil bolognese sauce (page 100), made with split orange lentils

salt and freshly ground black pepper

14 ounces lasagnette

1 Tbs olive oil, optional

sprigs of fresh oregano and freshly grated Parmesan cheese, to serve

Here, extra tomatoes, cinnamon and oregano are added to the basic sauce – and I think the sauce works better in this case made with split orange lentils rather than whole lentils.

1 First fill a large saucepan with 4 quarts of water and bring to a boil over high heat for the pasta.

2 Meanwhile, add the canned tomatoes, cinnamon and oregano to the bolognese sauce in a pan, breaking up the tomatoes with the spoon as you do so. Cook over a fairly low heat for 10–15 minutes. Check the sauce for seasoning, adding salt and pepper to taste if it needs it.

3 When the water in the saucepan boils, add the pasta along with a tablespoon of salt and give the pasta a quick stir. Briefly put the lid on until it starts to lift, showing that the water has come back to a boil, then let the pasta bubble away, uncovered, for about 8 minutes, or until it is tender but still has some bite to it.

4 Drain the pasta by tipping it all into a colander placed in the sink, then put it back into the still-warm pan. Either add the olive oil to the pasta, serve it on warm plates and spoon the sauce on top; or add the sauce directly to the pasta, toss gently and serve on warm plates. Garnish with fresh oregano and hand around the Parmesan.

FARFALLE WITH LENTIL BOLOGNESE SAUCE AND SPINACH Serves ❹

INGREDIENTS

14 ounces farfalle

salt

olive oil

3 cups tender spinach

1 quantity of lentil bolognese sauce (page 100)

freshly ground black pepper

fresh Parmesan cheese, cut in flakes or grated, to serve

Spinach and lentils go together like bread and cheese or strawberries and cream ... Put together with pasta, spinach and lentils make a wonderfully filling and tasty dish.

1 First fill a large saucepan with 4 quarts of water and bring to a boil over high heat for the pasta.

2 When the water boils, add the pasta along with a tablespoon of salt and give the pasta a quick stir. Briefly put the lid on until it starts to lift, showing that the water has come back to a boil, then let the pasta bubble away, uncovered, for about 8 minutes, or until it is tender but still has some bite to it.

3 Meanwhile, heat 1 tablespoon of olive oil in a saucepan, then add the spinach and stir-fry over high heat for 1–2 minutes, until the spinach has wilted. Remove from the heat and drain off any liquid.

4 Add the spinach to the bolognese sauce in a pan and heat through gently. Check the seasoning, adding salt and pepper to taste if it needs it.

5 Drain the pasta by tipping it all into a colander placed in the sink, then put it back into the still-warm pan. Either add 1 tablespoon of olive oil to the pasta, serve it on warm plates and spoon the sauce on top; or add the sauce directly to the pasta, toss gently and serve on warm plates. Scatter the Parmesan on top and serve at once.

TOMATO SAUCE Serves ❹

INGREDIENTS

1 Tbs olive oil

1 onion, peeled and chopped

2 garlic cloves, peeled and crushed

2 14-ounce cans tomatoes in juice

salt and freshly ground black pepper

A wonderful, basic standby, tomato sauce is quick to make and popular with most people. This is my favorite recipe for it – and also one of the simplest.

1 Heat the oil in a large saucepan and add the onion. Cover and cook gently for 10 minutes, until tender but not brown.

2 Add the garlic, stir well and cook for 1–2 minutes longer. Then stir in the tomatoes, together with their juice, breaking up the tomatoes with a wooden spoon.

3 Bring to a boil, then let the mixture simmer for 10–15 minutes until the liquid has disappeared and the sauce is thick.

4 Season with salt and pepper. It is important to season a tomato sauce with salt after it has cooked because salt added during cooking can toughen tomatoes.

•

For this delicate and delectable variation, use 2 pounds fresh tomatoes, skinned and coarsely chopped, instead of the canned tomatoes. Some fresh basil leaves, if available, torn into the sauce just before serving, make the perfect finishing touch.

PENNE WITH TOMATO SAUCE, CHILI AND RED BEANS Serves ❹

INGREDIENTS

14 ounces penne

salt

1 dried red chili, crumbled, or 1 fresh green chili, finely sliced

15 ounces canned red kidney beans, drained

1 quantity of tomato sauce (above)

freshly ground black pepper

squeeze of lemon juice, optional

1 Tbs olive oil, optional

several good sprigs of fresh cilantro, to serve

This is a substantial dish, and particularly good on a chilly day. To make it even more filling, you could serve it with warm bread rolls or garlic bread.

1 First fill a large saucepan with 4 quarts of water and bring to a boil over high heat for the pasta.

2 When the water boils, add the pasta along with a tablespoon of salt and give the pasta a quick stir. Briefly put the lid on until it starts to lift, showing that the water has come back to a boil, then let the pasta bubble away, uncovered, for about 8 minutes, or until it is tender but still has some bite to it.

3 Meanwhile, add the chili and beans to the tomato sauce in a pan and heat through gently, stirring from time to time. Check the seasoning, adding pepper, a squeeze of lemon juice and salt to taste if it needs it.

4 Drain the pasta by tipping it all into a colander placed in the sink, then put it back into the still-warm pan. Either add the olive oil to the pasta, serve it on warm plates and spoon the sauce on top; or add the sauce directly to the pasta, toss gently and serve on warm plates. Chop, snip or tear the cilantro over the top.

Penne with tomato sauce, chili and red beans

RIGATONI WITH TOMATO SAUCE, EGGPLANT AND MOZZARELLA   Serves ❹

INGREDIENTS

2 medium-sized eggplants

salt

14 ounces rigatoni

olive oil

1 quantity of tomato sauce
(page 106)

freshly ground black pepper

8 ounces fresh mozzarella cheese,
drained and cut into ¼-inch cubes

fresh basil leaves and flakes of
Parmesan cheese, to serve

You do not have to salt the eggplants in advance, but if you do, they will absorb less oil when you fry or broil them.

1 Cut the eggplants into thin slices. Sprinkle the slices with salt, put them into a colander and leave to drain for about an hour. Then rinse them under cold water and pat dry.

2 Fill a large saucepan with 4 quarts of water and bring to a boil over high heat for the pasta.

3 When the water boils, add the pasta along with a tablespoon of salt and give the pasta a quick stir. Briefly put the lid on until it starts to lift, showing that the water has come back to a boil, then let the pasta bubble away, uncovered, for about 8 minutes, or until it is tender but still has some bite to it.

4 Meanwhile, heat a little olive oil in a frying pan and sauté the eggplant slices until golden brown and tender; drain and blot

on paper towels. You will need to do more than one batch. Keep the eggplant slices warm under the broiler. Alternatively, brush the slices of eggplant with oil and put them under a hot broiler until they are tender and browned, turning them halfway through.

5 Heat the tomato sauce through gently. Check the seasoning, adding more – especially pepper – if it needs it. Stir two thirds of the mozzarella into the hot sauce so that it starts to melt.

6 Drain the pasta by tipping it all into a colander placed in the sink, then put it back into the still-warm pan. Either add the olive oil to the pasta, serve it on warm plates and spoon the sauce on top; or add the sauce directly to the pasta, toss gently and serve on warm plates. In either case, top each portion with some of the eggplant and the remaining mozzarella. Tear basil leaves over the top, scatter with flakes of Parmesan, and serve at once.

RUOTE DI CARRO WITH TOMATO SAUCE, SUN-DRIED TOMATOES AND ZUCCHINI Serves ❹

INGREDIENTS

14 ounces ruote di carro

salt

1 pound zucchini, cut into ¼ inch slices

2 Tbs of oil from the sun-dried tomatoes, optional (see below)

freshly ground black pepper

8 sun-dried tomatoes, chopped

1 quantity of tomato sauce (page 106)

squeeze of lemon juice, optional

1 Tbs olive oil, optional

fresh basil leaves and flakes of Parmesan cheese, to serve

Added sun-dried tomatoes intensify the flavor of the sauce and go well with the zucchini. This is also good made with farfalle or orecchiette — indeed any of the chunky pastas.

1 First fill a large saucepan with 4 quarts of water and bring to a boil over high heat for the pasta.

2 When the water boils, add the pasta along with a tablespoon of salt and give the pasta a quick stir. Briefly put the lid on until it starts to lift, showing that the water has come back to a boil, then let the pasta bubble away, uncovered, for about 8 minutes, or until it is tender but still has some bite to it.

3 Meanwhile, cook the zucchini, either by sautéing in the oil from the sun-dried tomatoes or, for a less rich result, in a little boiling water. Either way they will take 3–4 minutes. Drain the zucchini if necessary, season with salt and pepper and keep them warm.

4 Add the sun-dried tomatoes to the tomato sauce in a pan and heat through gently. Check the seasoning, adding a squeeze of lemon juice to taste if it needs it.

5 Drain the pasta by tipping it all into a colander placed in the sink, then put it back into the still-warm pan. Either add the olive oil to the pasta, serve it on warm plates and spoon the sauce on top; or add the sauce directly to the pasta, toss gently and serve on warm plates. Top with the zucchini and some grindings of black pepper, then tear basil leaves over the top, scatter with flakes of Parmesan and serve at once.

•

Sun-dried tomatoes can be bought in oil, as a purée or simply in their dried state. The ones in oil, and the paste, can be used as they are.

Dry sun-dried tomatoes need soaking for 30–60 minutes in hot water to plump them up, after which they can be used in the same way as tomatoes in oil. After soaking, they keep for no more than a day or two in the refrigerator, because they lack the protective layer of oil. They are, of course, low in fat, which can be an advantage.

PIPE RIGATE WITH TOMATO SAUCE, ARTICHOKE HEARTS AND SUN-DRIED TOMATOES   Serves ❹

INGREDIENTS

14 ounces pipe rigate

salt

14 ounces canned artichoke hearts, drained and sliced

8 sun-dried tomatoes, chopped

I quantity of tomato sauce (page 106)

freshly ground black pepper

squeeze of lemon juice, optional

I Tbs olive oil, optional

fresh basil leaves and flakes of Parmesan cheese, to serve

This is one of my favorite mixtures; I like to serve it with a leafy salad with a light vinaigrette dressing.

1 First fill a large saucepan with 4 quarts of water and bring to a boil over high heat for the pasta.

2 When the water boils, add the pasta along with a tablespoon of salt and give the pasta a quick stir. Briefly put the lid on until it starts to lift, showing that the water has come back to a boil, then let the pasta bubble away, uncovered, for about 8 minutes, or until it is tender but still has some bite to it.

3 Meanwhile, add the artichoke hearts and the sun-dried tomatoes to the tomato sauce in a pan and heat through gently. Check the seasoning, adding pepper, a squeeze of lemon juice and salt to taste if it needs it.

4 Drain the pasta by tipping it all into a colander placed in the sink, then put it back into the still-warm pan. Either add the olive oil to the pasta, serve it on warm plates and spoon the sauce on top; or add the sauce directly to the pasta, toss gently and serve on warm plates. Tear basil leaves over the top, scatter with flakes of Parmesan and serve at once.

SPAGHETTI WITH GINGER-TOMATO SAUCE, CHICKPEAS AND FRESH CILANTRO   Serves ❹

INGREDIENTS

14 ounces spaghetti

salt

walnut-sized piece of fresh ginger, grated

14 ounces canned chickpeas, drained

I quantity of tomato sauce (page 106)

freshly ground black pepper

squeeze of lemon juice, optional

I Tbs olive oil, optional

several good sprigs of fresh cilantro

Here the classic combination of pasta and chickpeas is enlivened with a ginger-tomato sauce and cilantro, to give the dish a slightly eastern flavor.

1 First fill a large saucepan with 4 quarts of water and bring to a boil over high heat for the pasta.

2 When the water boils, add the spaghetti, holding it straight up like a bunch of flowers and gently pushing it into the water as it softens. Add a tablespoon of salt and give the pasta a quick stir. Briefly put the lid on until it starts to lift, showing that the water has come back to a boil, then let the pasta bubble away, uncovered, for about 8 minutes, or until it is tender but still has some bite to it.

3 Meanwhile, stir the ginger and chickpeas into the tomato sauce in a pan, and heat through gently. Just before the pasta is ready, check the seasoning of the sauce, adding pepper, a squeeze of lemon juice and salt to taste if it needs it.

4 Drain the pasta by tipping it all into a colander placed in the sink, then put it back into the still-warm pan. Either add the olive oil to the pasta, serve it on warm plates and spoon the sauce on top; or add the sauce directly to the pasta, toss gently and serve on warm plates. Chop, snip or tear the cilantro over the top.

FARFALLE IN FRESH TOMATO SAUCE WITH FRESH BASIL Serves ❹

INGREDIENTS

14 ounces farfalle

salt

1 quantity of tomato sauce (page 106), made with fresh tomatoes

squeeze of lemon juice, optional

1 Tbs olive oil, optional

freshly ground black pepper

fresh basil leaves

So simple but, when well made, unbeatable.

1 First fill a large saucepan with 4 quarts of water and bring to a boil over high heat for the pasta.

2 When the water boils, add the pasta along with a tablespoon of salt and give the pasta a quick stir. Briefly put the lid on until it starts to lift, showing that the water has come back to a boil, then let the pasta bubble away, uncovered, for about 8 minutes, or until it is tender but still has some bite to it.

3 Heat the tomato sauce through gently. Check the seasoning, adding a squeeze of lemon juice to taste if it needs it.

4 Drain the pasta by tipping it all into a colander placed in the sink, then put it back into the still-warm pan. Either add the olive oil to the pasta, serve it on warm plates and spoon the sauce on top; or add the sauce directly to the pasta, toss gently and serve on warm plates. Grind a little pepper coarsely on top, tear the basil leaves over and serve at once.

LASAGNETTE WITH FRESH TOMATO SAUCE, BROILED GOLDEN BELL PEPPERS AND OLIVES Serves ❹

INGREDIENTS

2 large golden bell peppers

14 ounces lasagnette

salt

1 quantity of tomato sauce (page 106)

⅔ cup black olives

freshly ground black pepper

1 Tbs olive oil, optional

fresh basil leaves, to serve

Another mixture of ingredients that seems to go well with almost any type of pasta; it's also very good with any of the chunky ones. You can use red instead of golden peppers.

1 First fill a large saucepan with 4 quarts of water and bring to a boil over high heat for the pasta.

2 Meanwhile, prepare the bell peppers by cutting them into quarters and placing, skin-side (shiny side) up, on a broiler pan. Put under high heat for 10–15 minutes, until the skin has blistered and blackened in places. Cover the peppers with a plate and leave until cool enough to handle, then remove the skin, stem and seeds, and cut the flesh into slices. Keep the slices warm.

3 When the water in the saucepan boils, add the pasta along with a tablespoon of salt and give the pasta a quick stir. Briefly put the lid on until it starts to lift, showing that the water has come back to a boil, then let the pasta bubble away, uncovered, for about 8 minutes, or until it is tender but still has some bite to it.

4 Heat the tomato sauce through gently. Add the olives and check the seasoning, adding pepper to taste if it needs it.

5 Drain the pasta by tipping it all into a colander placed in the sink, then put it back into the still-warm pan. Either add the olive oil to the pasta, serve it on warm plates and spoon the sauce on top; or add the sauce directly to the pasta, toss gently and serve on warm plates. Top with the golden bell peppers and tear the basil leaves over.

LASAGNETTE WITH MASCARPONE AND MUSHROOMS IN TOMATO SAUCE Serves ❹

INGREDIENTS

14 ounces lasagnette

salt

2 Tbs butter

4 cups mushrooms, cleaned and sliced

2 garlic cloves, peeled and crushed

½ cup mascarpone cheese (or you could use a low-fat cream cheese)

1 quantity of tomato sauce (page 106)

freshly ground black pepper

1 Tbs olive oil, optional

fresh basil leaves and flakes of Parmesan cheese, to serve

I like frilly lasagnette for this, but if it is unavailable, substitute almost any other pasta that you fancy, long or short. This is a very easygoing mixture and does not depend on any particular type of pasta for flavor or effect.

1 First fill a large saucepan with 4 quarts of water and bring to a boil over high heat for the pasta.

2 When the water boils, add the pasta along with a tablespoon of salt and give the pasta a quick stir. Briefly put the lid on until it starts to lift, showing that the water has come back to a boil, then let the pasta bubble away, uncovered, for about 8 minutes, or until it is tender but still has some bite to it.

3 Meanwhile, cook the mushrooms: melt the butter in a medium saucepan, add the mushrooms and garlic and cook for 4–5 minutes, or until they are tender and any liquid has disappeared, stirring from time to time.

4 Add the mascarpone cheese to the tomato sauce in a pan and heat through gently, stirring until the cheese has melted. Then add the mushrooms and check the seasoning, adding salt and pepper to taste if it needs it.

5 Drain the pasta by tipping it all into a colander placed in the sink, then put it back into the still-warm pan. Either add the olive oil to the pasta, serve it on warm plates and spoon the sauce on top; or add the sauce directly to the pasta, toss gently and serve on warm plates. Tear some basil leaves over, scatter with flakes of Parmesan and serve as soon as possible.

RIGATONI WITH TOMATO SAUCE, BROILED FENNEL AND OLIVES Serves ❹

INGREDIENTS

1 pound fennel bulbs, trimmed, reserving any feathery leaves, and sliced into eighths

olive oil

14 ounces rigatoni

salt

1 quantity of tomato sauce (page 106)

freshly ground black pepper

squeeze of lemon juice, optional

⅔ cup black olives

Juicy slices of broiled fennel combine well with the tomato sauce and olives. Serve this with some warm crusty bread.

1 First fill a large saucepan with 4 quarts of water and bring to a boil over high heat for the pasta.

2 Meanwhile, parboil the fennel in a little boiling water for 4–5 minutes, until just tender, and then drain well. Brush the fennel lightly all over with olive oil, put it in a single layer on a broiler pan or cookie sheet that will fit under your broiler, and broil under high heat until tender and tinged with brown: 4–5 minutes. Keep the fennel warm.

3 When the water in the saucepan boils, add the pasta along with a tablespoon of salt and give the pasta a quick stir. Briefly put the lid on until it starts to lift, showing that the water has come back to a boil, then let the pasta bubble away, uncovered, for about 8 minutes, or until it is tender but still has some bite to it.

4 Heat the tomato sauce through gently. Check the seasoning, adding pepper, a squeeze of lemon juice and salt to taste if it needs it.

5 Drain the pasta by tipping it all into a colander placed in the sink, then put it back into the still-warm pan, then either add 1 tablespoon of olive oil to the pasta, serve it on warm plates and spoon the sauce on top; or add the sauce directly to the pasta, toss gently and serve on warm plates. Either way, top with the broiled fennel and black olives and serve at once.

SPAGHETTI PUTTANESCA Serves ❹

Well known but none the less delicious, this "whore's pasta" is spicy and piquant.

1 First fill a large saucepan with 4 quarts of water and bring to a boil over high heat for the pasta.

2 When the water boils, add the spaghetti, holding it straight up like a bunch of flowers and gently pushing it into the water as it softens. Add a tablespoon of salt and give the pasta a quick stir. Briefly put the lid on until it starts to lift, showing that the water has come back to a boil, then let the pasta bubble away, uncovered, for about 8 minutes, or until it is tender but still has some bite to it.

3 Meanwhile, add the garlic, sun-dried tomato paste, capers, olives and oregano to the tomato sauce in a pan and heat through gently, stirring from time to time. Check the seasoning, adding more – especially pepper – if you think it needs it.

4 Drain the pasta by tipping it all into a colander placed in the sink, then put it back into the still-warm pan. Either add the olive oil to the pasta, serve it on warm plates and spoon the sauce on top; or add the sauce directly to the pasta, toss gently and serve on warm plates.

PENNE ARRABBIATA Serves ❹

A lovely, punchy, classic pasta dish; you can vary the heat by adding more or less chili.

1 First fill a large saucepan with 4 quarts of water and bring to a boil over high heat for the pasta.

2 When the water boils, add the pasta along with a tablespoon of salt and give the pasta a quick stir. Briefly put the lid on until it starts to lift, showing that the water has come back to a boil, then let the pasta bubble away, uncovered, for about 8 minutes, or until it is tender but still has some bite to it.

3 Meanwhile, add the red chili and the sun-dried tomato paste to the tomato sauce in a pan and heat through gently, stirring from time to time. Check the seasoning, adding salt and pepper to taste if it needs it.

4 Drain the pasta by tipping it all into a colander placed in the sink, then put it back into the still-warm pan. Either add the olive oil to the pasta, serve it on warm plates and spoon the sauce on top; or add the sauce directly to the pasta, toss gently and serve on warm plates.

CONCHIGLIE WITH CORN AND TOMATO SAUCE Serves ❹

INGREDIENTS

14 ounces conchiglie

salt

1½ cups corn, cut from the cob, frozen or canned

1 quantity of tomato sauce (page 106)

freshly ground black pepper

squeeze of lemon juice, optional

1 Tbs olive oil, optional

A simple mixture that is popular with children. You can use fresh, frozen or canned corn. I like to serve it with salad; a mixture of grated carrot and shredded cabbage, lightly dressed, is also well liked by children.

1 First fill a large saucepan with 4 quarts of water and bring to a boil over high heat for the pasta.

2 When the water boils, add the pasta along with a tablespoon of salt and give the pasta a quick stir. Briefly put the lid on until it starts to lift, showing that the water has come back to a boil, then let the pasta bubble away, uncovered, for about 8 minutes, or until it is tender but still has some bite to it.

3 Meanwhile, cook the corn in a little boiling water for 3–4 minutes, or until it is just tender, then drain and add to the tomato sauce in a pan.

4 Heat the tomato sauce through gently. Check the seasoning, adding pepper, a squeeze of lemon juice and salt to taste if it needs it.

5 Drain the pasta by tipping it all into a colander placed in the sink, then put it back into the still-warm pan. Either add the olive oil to the pasta, serve it on warm plates and spoon the sauce on top; or add the sauce directly to the pasta, toss gently and serve on warm plates.

. . . .

FUSILLI WITH CREAMY TOMATO SAUCE, GREEN PEAS, BASIL AND PARMESAN Serves ❹

INGREDIENTS

14 ounces fusilli

salt

1 pound shelled fresh peas or frozen petits pois

1 quantity of tomato sauce (page 106)

¼ cup light cream

freshly ground black pepper

1 Tbs olive oil, optional

fresh basil leaves and flakes of Parmesan cheese

The cream reduces the acidity of the sauce, making this a very mellow dish. Soy cream also works well.

1 First fill a large saucepan with 4 quarts of water and bring to a boil over high heat for the pasta.

2 When the water boils, add the pasta along with a tablespoon of salt and give the pasta a quick stir. Briefly put the lid on until it starts to lift, showing that the water has come back to a boil, then let the pasta bubble away, uncovered, for about 8 minutes, or until it is tender but still has some bite to it.

3 Add the peas to the tomato sauce in a pan and place over low heat, to heat through both the peas and the sauce. Just before the pasta is done, add the cream to the sauce and check the seasoning, adding salt and pepper to taste if it needs it.

4 Drain the pasta by tipping it all into a colander placed in the sink, then put it back into the still-warm pan. Either add the olive oil to the pasta, serve it on warm plates and spoon the sauce on top; or add the sauce directly to the pasta, toss gently and serve on warm plates. Tear basil leaves over the top, scatter with Parmesan and serve at once.

117

Lasagne and Other Baked Pasta Dishes

This section contains a variety of dishes linked by the fact that after they have been assembled they need to be baked in the oven or cooked under the broiler. Some of them are quite simple; others take a bit longer to put together. The hard work can often be done well in advance, however, making many of them perfect for informal entertaining.

Anyone who has had to cater for a crowd will know the advantages of dishes such as lasagne – you can make them in advance, bake them when you are ready and know that they will not spoil if the meal is a little delayed. So I have included a good selection of different types of lasagne, some of which are a little out of the ordinary. They all freeze well, too. Freeze them before baking, and remember to get them out of the freezer the night before to allow time to thaw.

Pasta bakes serve a rather similar function to lasagne and make a nice variation on that theme. These freeze well, too, and, like lasagne, need only be accompanied by a salad or a very simple cooked vegetable, such as green beans or spinach. Again, they make a practical choice for feeding a crowd. One of the more unusual pasta bakes is the terrine, which is easy to make and stunning to look at. It is good either as an appetizer or a light main course.

Also included in this section are some vegetable dishes, in which pasta is used to make a tasty stuffing, and some delicious cannelloni bakes.

RED BEAN LASAGNE Serves ❻

INGREDIENTS

1 Tbs olive oil

1 onion, peeled and very finely chopped

1 large garlic clove, peeled and crushed

14 ounces canned tomatoes

2 15-ounce cans red kidney beans, drained and rinsed

2 heaping Tbs sun-dried tomato paste

½–1 tsp chili powder

salt and freshly ground black pepper

5–6 ounces no-cook lasagne verde

1 quantity of béchamel sauce (page 90)

⅔ cup freshly grated Parmesan cheese

This moist and delicious lasagne is high in protein thanks to its ideal pasta-and-legume combination. It is good with a leafy salad or a lightly cooked vegetable, such as green beans or broccoli.

1 Set the oven to 400°F. Grease a casserole dish or roasting pan about 8 x 12 inches and at least 2½ inches deep.

2 Heat the oil in a medium-sized saucepan and sauté the onion for 5 minutes with a lid on the pan. Then add the garlic and cook for a few seconds longer. Add the tomatoes, breaking them up with a wooden spoon, and then the red kidney beans. bring to a boil, then leave to simmer, uncovered, for 10–15 minutes, until thick. Add the sun-dried tomato paste, chili powder and salt and pepper to taste.

3 Rinse the lasagne sheets under cold water, then arrange sheets of lasagne in the base of the dish, to cover it. On top of this put a layer of béchamel sauce, then half the red bean mixture. Top this with another layer of lasagne, then half of the remaining béchamel and the rest of the red kidney bean mixture. Finish with a layer of lasagne followed by the remainder of the béchamel sauce. Scatter the Parmesan cheese on top.

4 Bake the lasagne in the oven for 35–40 minutes, until the pasta is tender and the top is golden brown.

SPINACH LASAGNE Serves ❻

INGREDIENTS

4 Tbs butter

1½ pounds frozen spinach, defrosted, or fresh spinach, washed

1 cup ricotta cheese

2 garlic cloves, peeled and crushed

1½ cups freshly grated Parmesan cheese

freshly grated nutmeg

salt and freshly ground black pepper

5–6 ounces no-cook lasagne

1 quantity of béchamel sauce (page 90)

I am always making different versions of this lasagne because it is so popular with my daughter and her friends. This is my latest.

1 Set the oven to 400°F. Grease a casserole dish or roasting pan about 8 x 12 inches and at least 2½ inches deep.

2 Melt the butter in a large saucepan over moderate heat and put in the spinach. Cook, uncovered, for 5–6 minutes, or until the spinach is tender, pushing it down into the pan and chopping it with the end of a metal spatula as it cooks. Unless you have a very large saucepan, you may need to cook the spinach in two batches, using half the butter for each batch.

3 Mix the spinach with the ricotta cheese, garlic, half the Parmesan, and nutmeg, salt and pepper to taste.

4 Rinse the lasagne sheets under cold water, then arrange half of the sheets in the base of the dish, to cover it. Pour in a little of the béchamel sauce. Put in half the spinach mixture, then another layer of béchamel sauce and then the remaining spinach. Follow with the remaining lasagne and then the rest of the béchamel sauce. Scatter the rest of the Parmesan cheese on top.

5 Bake the lasagne in the oven for 35–40 minutes, until the pasta is tender and the top golden brown.

VEGETARIAN LASAGNE AL FORNO Serves ❻

INGREDIENTS

5–6 ounces no-cook lasagne verde

1 quantity of béchamel sauce (page 90)

⅔ cup freshly grated Parmesan cheese

FOR THE MUSHROOM BOLOGNESE SAUCE:

2 Tbs olive oil

1 onion, peeled and very finely chopped

1 pound mushrooms

1 large garlic clove, peeled and crushed

14 ounces canned tomatoes

2 Tbs sherry or 3–4 Tbs red wine

2 heaping Tbs sun-dried tomato paste

1 tsp dried basil

2 tsp black olive paste or pitted and mashed black olives

salt and freshly ground black pepper

Based on a recipe I created for my book *The New Simply Delicious*, this is a vegetarian version of the classic Lasagne al Forno, which does not use lentils to replace the meat but rather a light and tasty mushroom sauce. A delectable dish.

1 Set the oven to 400°F. Grease a casserole dish or roasting pan about 8 x 12 inches and at least 2½ inches deep.

2 Make the mushroom bolognese sauce: heat the oil in a medium-sized saucepan and sauté the onion for 5 minutes with a lid on the pan. Meanwhile, wipe the mushrooms with a clean damp cloth, then chop them up as finely as possible – they can be done in a food processor, but take care not to purée them completely.

3 Add the mushrooms to the onion along with the garlic (if you are chopping the mushrooms in a food processor the whole peeled garlic clove can be crushed by putting it in with them) and sauté for a further 5 minutes, browning lightly and stirring often.

4 Add the tomatoes, sherry or wine, sun-dried tomato paste and basil. Mix well, then put a lid on the pan and leave the sauce to simmer for 25–30 minutes, until thick. Add the olive paste and salt and pepper to taste.

5 Rinse the lasagne sheets under cold water, then arrange sheets of lasagne in the base of the dish, to cover it. On top of this put first a layer of half the mushroom sauce, then one of béchamel sauce, using a third of the sauce. Top this with another layer of lasagne, then the rest of the mushroom sauce followed by béchamel. Finish with a layer of lasagne followed by the remainder of the béchamel. Scatter the Parmesan on top.

6 Bake the lasagne in the oven for 35–40 minutes, until the pasta is tender and the top golden brown.

CORN, RICOTTA, TOMATO AND CHEDDAR CHEESE LASAGNE Serves ❻

INGREDIENTS

2 cups ricotta cheese

1¾ cups frozen or canned corn

1 cup Cheddar cheese, grated

salt and freshly ground black pepper

5–6 ounces no-cook lasagne verde

2 quantities of tomato sauce (page 106)

Another dish that is popular with the younger age group, and quite quick to make.

1 Set the oven to 400°F. Grease a casserole dish or roasting pan about 8 x 12 inches and at least 2½ inches deep.

2 Mix the ricotta cheese with the corn (no need to cook it) and half the cheese. Season with salt and pepper.

3 To assemble the lasagne, rinse the lasagne sheets under cold water, then arrange sheets of lasagne in the base of the dish, to cover it. Pour in a little of the tomato sauce.

Put in half the corn mixture, then another layer of lasagne and some more tomato sauce. Follow with the remaining corn mixture, lasagne and the rest of the tomato sauce. Scatter the remaining Cheddar cheese on top.

4 Bake the lasagne in the oven for 35–40 minutes, until the pasta is tender and the top golden brown.

MUSHROOM AND GARLIC CREAM CHEESE LASAGNE Serves ❻

INGREDIENTS

2 Tbs olive oil

1 onion, peeled and finely chopped

1½ pounds mushrooms, washed and sliced

1 large garlic clove, peeled and crushed

1 cup full-fat or reduced fat garlic cream cheese

salt and freshly ground black pepper

5–6 ounces no-cook lasagne verde

2 quantities of tomato sauce (page 106)

⅔ cup freshly grated Parmesan cheese

A mixed salad goes well with this lasagne; vary the types of mushroom used if you can get hold of some exciting ones.

1 Set the oven to 400°F. Grease a casserole dish or roasting pan about 8 x 12 inches and at least 2½ inches deep.

2 Heat the oil in a medium-sized saucepan and sauté the onion for 5 minutes with a lid on the pan. Then add the sliced mushrooms to the onion along with the garlic and sauté for a further 5–10 minutes, until the mushrooms are tender and any liquid they have produced has boiled away. Remove the pan from the heat, stir in the cream cheese and season with salt and pepper.

3 Rinse the lasagne sheets under cold water, then arrange sheets of lasagne in the base of the dish, to cover it. On top of this put first a layer of tomato sauce, then half the mushroom sauce, followed by a layer of lasagne and another of tomato sauce. Top this with the remaining mushroom mixture, the rest of the lasagne and a final layer of tomato sauce. Scatter the Parmesan cheese on top.

4 Bake the lasagne in the oven for 35–40 minutes, until the pasta is tender and the top golden brown.

Corn, ricotta, tomato and Cheddar cheese lasagne

ROASTED ASPARAGUS AND FRESH HERB LASAGNE Serves ❻

INGREDIENTS

2 bunches of asparagus, tough ends removed and the spears cut in half

2 Tbs olive oil

4 Tbs chopped fresh herbs: parsley, chervil, chives

salt and freshly ground black pepper

5–6 ounces no-cook lasagne

1 quantity of béchamel sauce (page 90)

⅔ cup freshly grated Parmesan cheese

This lasagne is light and fresh; just right with a summery salad of young vegetables and some chilled white wine.

1 Set the oven to 400°F. Grease a casserole dish or roasting pan about 8 x 12 inches and at least 2½ inches deep.

2 Toss the asparagus in the oil, using your fingers to make sure that each piece is coated. Put the asparagus into a shallow roasting pan and roast in the oven for 20 minutes. Then remove from the oven and add the herbs and salt and pepper to taste.

3 Rinse the lasagne sheets under cold water, then arrange sheets of lasagne in the base of the dish, to cover it. On top of this put first a layer of béchamel sauce, then half the asparagus followed by a layer of lasagne and more cream sauce. Top this with the rest of the asparagus. Finish with a layer of lasagne followed by the remainder of the béchamel sauce and scatter the Parmesan cheese on top.

4 Bake the lasagne in the oven for 35–40 minutes, until the pasta is tender and the top golden brown.

RED ONION AND GOAT CHEESE LASAGNE Serves ❻

INGREDIENTS

2 Tbs olive oil

2 Tbs butter

1½ pounds red onions, peeled and sliced

1 large garlic clove, peeled and crushed

salt and freshly ground black pepper

5–6 ounces no-cook lasagne verde

1 quantity of béchamel sauce (page 90)

7-ounce goat cheese log, sliced into thin rounds

Warming and good in winter, this lasagne can also be made with regular onions instead of red ones. The important thing is to let them cook for long enough so that they become sweet and melting.

1 Set the oven to 400°F. Grease a casserole dish or roasting pan about 8 x 12 inches and at least 2½ inches deep.

2 Heat the oil and butter in a large saucepan and sauté the onions and garlic gently for 30 minutes, until they are very tender, stirring from time to time. Season with salt and freshly ground black pepper.

3 Rinse the lasagne sheets under cold water, then arrange sheets of lasagne in the base of the dish, to cover it. On top of this put first a layer of béchamel sauce, then half the onions. Top this with another layer of lasagne, then more béchamel sauce, a layer of half of the goat cheese and the rest of the onions. Finish with a layer of lasagne followed by the remainder of the béchamel and the rest of the goat cheese.

4 Bake the lasagne in the oven for 35–40 minutes, until the pasta is tender and the top golden brown.

BROCCOLI AND BRIE LASAGNE Serves ❻

INGREDIENTS

4 cups prepared broccoli, cut into small pieces

salt and freshly ground black pepper

5–6 ounces no-cook lasagne

1 quantity of béchamel sauce (page 90), or 2 quantities of tomato sauce (page 106)

7 ounces Brie cheese, thinly sliced

Serve this with a tomato salad, or some roasted tomatoes that can be done in the oven with the lasagne.

1 Set the oven to 400°F. Grease a casserole dish or roasting pan about 8 x 12 inches and at least 2½ inches deep.

2 Cook the broccoli in a little boiling water for 4–5 minutes until it is tender; drain and season with salt and pepper.

3 Rinse the lasagne sheets under cold water, then arrange sheets of lasagne in the base of the dish, to cover it. On top of this put first a layer of sauce, then half the broccoli. Top this with another layer of lasagne, then more sauce, a layer of half of the Brie cheese and the rest of the broccoli. Finish with a layer of lasagne followed by the remainder of the sauce and the rest of the Brie cheese.

4 Bake the lasagne in the oven for 35–40 minutes, until the pasta is tender and the top golden brown.

LEEK, OLIVE, FETA AND SUN-DRIED TOMATO LASAGNE Serves ❻

INGREDIENTS

1½ pounds leeks, trimmed and cut into ¼-inch slices

2 Tbs oil from the sun-dried tomatoes, optional

2 ounces sun-dried tomatoes, chopped

⅓ cup pitted and chopped black olives

1 Tbs chopped fresh oregano, optional

salt and freshly ground black pepper

5–6 ounces no-cook lasagne

1 quantity of béchamel sauce (page 90)

7 ounces feta cheese, thinly sliced

One of my favorite combinations of flavors and textures – leeks, sun-dried tomatoes and olives – is here in this lasagne. Good with a green salad.

1 Set the oven to 400°F. Grease a casserole dish or roasting pan about 8 x 12 inches and at least 2½ inches deep.

2 Next cook the leeks, either by sautéing in the oil from the sun-dried tomatoes or, for a less rich result, in a little boiling water. Either way they will take about 6 minutes. Drain the leeks if necessary and add the sun-dried tomatoes, olives, oregano if using, and salt and pepper to taste.

3 Rinse the lasagne sheets under cold water, then arrange sheets of lasagne in the base of the dish, to cover it. On top of this put first a layer of béchamel sauce, then half the leek mixture. Top this with another layer of lasagne, then more sauce, a layer of half of the feta cheese and the rest of the leek mixture. Finish with a layer of lasagne followed by the remainder of the sauce and the rest of the feta cheese.

4 Bake the lasagne in the oven for 35–40 minutes, until the pasta is tender and the top golden brown.

PUMPKIN AND GOAT CHEESE LASAGNE Serves ❻

INGREDIENTS

2 Tbs olive oil

2 Tbs butter

1 onion, peeled and chopped

3½ pounds pumpkin, skin and seeds removed, flesh cut into ½-inch dice (weight after skin and seeds taken away about 2½ pounds)

1 large garlic clove, peeled and crushed

salt and freshly ground black pepper

5–6 ounces no-cook lasagne verde

1 quantity of béchamel sauce (page 90)

7-ounce goat cheese log, sliced into thin rounds

An excellent combination of flavors and textures, this is a lovely lasagne for the cooler days of autumn. You can use a tomato sauce (see page 106) in place of the béchamel sauce, if you prefer, for a very colorful result.

1 Set the oven to 400°F. Grease a casserole dish or roasting pan about 8 x 12 inches and at least 2½ inches deep.

2 Heat the oil and butter in a large saucepan and sauté the onion gently for 5 minutes with a lid on the pan. Then add the pumpkin and garlic, and mix so that the pumpkin is coated with the butter and oil. Cover the pan and cook slowly for 15–20 minutes, until the pumpkin is tender. Season to taste with salt and pepper.

3 Rinse the lasagne sheets under cold water, then arrange sheets of lasagne in the base of the dish, to cover it. On top of this put first a layer of béchamel sauce, then half the pumpkin. Top this with another layer of lasagne, then more béchamel sauce, a layer of half of the goat cheese and the rest of the pumpkin. Finish with a layer of lasagne followed by the remainder of the béchamel and the rest of the goat cheese.

4 Bake the lasagne in the oven for 35–40 minutes, until the pasta is tender and the top golden brown.

SPAGHETTI, TOMATO, CHEESE AND MUSHROOM BAKE Serves ❹

INGREDIENTS

6 ounces spaghetti

salt

1 Tbs olive oil

1 onion, peeled and chopped

8 ounces mushrooms, washed and chopped

1 garlic clove, peeled and crushed

14 ounces canned tomatoes

1 egg, beaten

1 cup Cheddar or Gruyère cheese, grated

1 Tbs chopped fresh oregano

freshly ground black pepper

¼ cup fresh bread crumbs

⅓ cup freshly grated Parmesan cheese

This is a good recipe to serve a crowd. It can be made well in advance – particularly useful when you have a lot of guests.

1 First fill a large saucepan with 4 quarts of water and bring to a boil over high heat for the pasta.

2 Set the oven to 400°F. Grease a casserole dish or roasting pan about 8 x 12 inches and at least 2½ inches deep.

3 When the water in the saucepan boils, add the spaghetti, holding it straight up like a bunch of flowers and gently pushing it into the water as it softens. Add a tablespoon of salt and give the pasta a quick stir. Briefly put the lid on until it starts to lift, showing that the water has come back to a boil, then let the pasta bubble away, uncovered, for about 8 minutes, or until it is tender but still has some bite to it. Drain the spaghetti.

4 Meanwhile, heat the oil in a medium-sized saucepan and put in the onion; cover and sauté for 5 minutes. Then add the mushrooms, garlic and tomatoes and cook, uncovered, for a further 10 minutes, until the onions and mushrooms are tender.

5 Add the egg to the vegetable mixture and stir well over the heat for a minute or two until the egg has cooked. Remove from the heat and add the spaghetti, along with the Cheddar or Gruyère cheese. Season with oregano and salt and pepper.

6 Spoon the spaghetti mixture into the ovenproof dish, scatter with the bread crumbs and Parmesan and bake for about 30 minutes, until golden brown and crisp on top.

MEDITERRANEAN BAKE WITH CONCHIGLIE Serves ❹

INGREDIENTS

2 Tbs olive oil

1 onion, peeled and chopped

1 fennel bulb

1 garlic clove, peeled and crushed

1 red bell pepper, de-seeded and chopped

1 yellow bell pepper, de-seeded and chopped

14 ounces canned tomatoes

8 ounces conchiglie

salt

⅓ cup black olives, optional

freshly ground black pepper

½ cup Gruyère cheese, grated

Another useful recipe that can be made in advance if you wish. In this case, it is best baked in the oven, to heat it through thoroughly. It needs about 30 minutes at 400°F.

Serve with a leafy salad – for instance, baby spinach leaves and thinly sliced purple onions in a mustardy vinaigrette – and warm, crusty bread.

1 First fill a large saucepan with 4 quarts of water and bring to a boil over high heat for the pasta.

2 Meanwhile, heat 1 tablespoon of the oil in a medium-sized saucepan and put in the onion; cover and sauté for 5 minutes.

3 With a sharp knife, pare away any tough, outer layers of the fennel. Then slice the fennel and add to the onion, along with the garlic, red and yellow bell peppers and tomatoes. Cook, uncovered, for 15–20 minutes, or until all the vegetables are tender.

4 When the water in the saucepan boils, add the pasta along with a tablespoon of salt and give the pasta a quick stir. Briefly put the lid on until it starts to lift, showing that the water has come back to a boil, then let the pasta bubble away, uncovered, for about 8 minutes, or until it is tender but still has some bite to it.

5 Set the broiler to high. Drain the pasta and put it into a shallow dish that will fit under the broiler. Add the remaining tablespoon of olive oil and toss well.

6 Add the olives, if using, to the vegetable mixture, season the mixture with salt and pepper, and then pour this over the pasta. Top with a layer of Gruyère cheese, then place under the broiler until the cheese has melted and is golden brown, and the dish is piping hot right through. Serve at once.

PASTA TERRINE Serves ❻ to ❽

INGREDIENTS

butter for greasing

8 ounces rigatoni

salt

1 Tbs olive oil

1 onion, peeled and chopped

1 garlic clove, peeled and crushed

1 green bell pepper, de-seeded and chopped

14 ounces canned tomatoes

1 cup fine soft bread crumbs

6 Tbs sun-dried tomato paste

1 Tbs chopped fresh oregano

2 eggs, beaten

1⅓ cups freshly grated Parmesan cheese

freshly ground black pepper

An impressive dish that is very easy to make and serves 6 to 8 people. Serve it cold, in slices, on a pool of tomato sauce or with a mixture of mayonnaise, low-fat plain yogurt and green peppercorns. Or eat it hot, in thick slices, with lightly cooked vegetables or a crisp salad.

1 First fill a large saucepan with 4 quarts of water and bring to a boil over high heat for the pasta.

2 Set the oven to 350°F. Line a 2-pound loaf pan with a sheet of wax paper to cover the base and extend up the narrow sides. Grease with butter.

3 When the water in the saucepan boils, add the pasta along with a tablespoon of salt and give the pasta a quick stir. Briefly put the lid on until it starts to lift, showing that the water has come back to a boil, then let the pasta bubble away, uncovered, for about 8 minutes, or until it is tender but still has some bite to it. Drain the pasta.

4 Meanwhile, heat the oil in a medium-sized saucepan and add the onion; cover and sauté for 5 minutes. Then add the garlic, green bell pepper and tomatoes and cook, uncovered, for a further 10–15 minutes, until the onion and pepper are tender and the mixture is thick. Remove from the heat.

5 Add the pasta to the tomato mixture in the pan, along with the bread crumbs, sun-dried tomato paste, oregano, eggs, three-quarters of the cheese, and salt and pepper to taste. Mix well, then pour into the prepared loaf pan.

6 Scatter with the remaining Parmesan and bake for about 45 minutes, until the terrine is firm to the touch and a knife inserted into the center comes out clean. Cool for a minute or two in the pan, then slip a knife around the edges, invert the pan over a plate and turn the terrine out. Serve in slices.

CHILI PASTA BAKE WITH RED BEANS Serves ❹

INGREDIENTS

8 ounces penne

salt

2 Tbs olive oil

1 onion, peeled and chopped

1 garlic clove, peeled and crushed

1 red bell pepper, de-seeded and chopped

14 ounces canned tomatoes

15 ounces canned red kidney beans, drained and rinsed

2 Tbs sun-dried tomato paste

½–1 tsp chili powder

freshly ground black pepper

1 cup fresh bread crumbs

This dish is useful when you want to make something ahead of time that is tasty and filling. Serve it with a salad of avocado and green leaves in a light vinaigrette dressing, and some bread or tortilla chips.

1 First fill a large saucepan with 4 quarts of water and bring to a boil over high heat for the pasta.

2 Set the oven to 400°F. Grease a casserole dish or roasting pan about 8 x 12 inches and at least 2½ inches deep.

3 When the water in the saucepan boils, add the pasta along with a tablespoon of salt and give the pasta a quick stir. Briefly put the lid on until it starts to lift, showing that the water has come back to a boil, then let the pasta bubble away, uncovered, for about 8 minutes, or until it is tender but still has some bite to it. Drain the pasta.

4 Meanwhile, heat 1 tablespoon of the oil in a medium-sized saucepan and put in the onion; cover and cook for minutes. Then add the garlic, red bell pepper, tomatoes and beans, and cook, uncovered, for a further 10–15 minutes, until the onion and pepper are tender and the mixture is thick. Remove from the heat.

5 Add the sun-dried tomato paste, then season the mixture with chili powder to taste, salt and pepper. Add the pasta, and toss well in the sauce.

6 Spoon the mixture into the prepared dish. Mix the bread crumbs with the remaining olive oil and scatter them on top. Bake for about 30 minutes, until the crumbs are browned and crisp.

PASTA, LENTIL AND VEGETABLE BAKE WITH FETA CHEESE AND THYME Serves ❹

INGREDIENTS

⅓ cup green or brown lentils, or a 14-ounce can

1 cup any small pasta: macaroni, penne, rigatoni

salt

2 Tbs olive oil

1 onion, peeled and chopped

1 garlic clove, peeled and crushed

2 large carrots, peeled and cut into ¼ inch slices

2 stalks of celery

8 ounces leeks, trimmed and cut into ¼-inch slices

2 Tbs sun-dried tomato paste

1 Tbs chopped thyme

4 Tbs chopped parsley

7 ounces feta cheese, crumbled

freshly ground black pepper

2–4 Tbs fresh bread crumbs

This is filling and nutritious – good for a chilly winter's day. Buttery cooked kale or cabbage goes well with it, or baked potatoes, which can be done in the oven at the same time (start them off first).

1 If you are using dried lentils, put them into a saucepan with plenty of cold water to cover them well, bring them to a boil, then leave them to simmer gently for 40–45 minutes, until tender.

2 Fill a saucepan with 2 quarts of water and bring to a boil over high heat for the pasta.

3 When the water in the saucepan boils, add the pasta along with a tablespoon of salt and give the pasta a quick stir. Briefly put the lid on until it starts to lift, showing that the water has come back to a boil, then let the pasta bubble away, uncovered, for about 8 minutes, or until it is tender but still has some bite to it. Drain the pasta.

4 Set the oven to 400°F. Grease a casserole dish or roasting pan about 8 x 12 inches and at least 2½ inches deep.

5 Meanwhile, heat the oil in a medium-sized saucepan and add the onion; cover and sauté for 5 minutes. Add the garlic, carrots and celery; cover and cook gently for 5 minutes. Then add the leeks, cover and cook for a further 10 minutes, until all the vegetables are tender.

6 Drain the lentils and add to the pasta, along with the vegetable mixture, sun-dried tomato paste, thyme and parsley. Crumble in half the feta. Mix well and season with salt and pepper.

7 Spoon the mixture into the prepared casserole dish or roasting pan and scatter the remaining feta cheese and the bread crumbs on top. Then bake the casserole for about 30 minutes, until the topping is golden brown.

MACARONI, CHEESE AND TOMATO BAKE Serves ❹

INGREDIENTS

8 ounces macaroni

salt

1 tsp mustard

1 egg, separated

1½ cups grated Cheddar cheese

1 quantity of béchamel sauce
(page 90)

freshly ground black pepper

1 pound fresh tomatoes, sliced

A new version of an old favorite, this is very good with a lightly cooked green vegetable or a salad.

1 First fill a saucepan with 4 quarts of water and bring to a boil over high heat for the pasta.

2 Set the oven to 400°F. Grease a casserole dish or roasting pan about 8 x 12 inches and at least 2½ inches deep.

3 When the water boils, add the pasta with a tablespoon of salt and give the pasta a stir. Briefly put the lid on until it starts to lift, showing that the water has come back to a boil. Let the pasta bubble away, uncovered, for about 8 minutes, or until it is tender but still has some bite to it. Drain the pasta.

4 Stir the mustard, egg yolk and ½ cup of the cheese into the béchamel sauce.

5 Whisk the egg white until it is stiff but not dry, then fold into the macaroni mixture, along with salt and pepper to taste.

6 Pour the mixture into the prepared dish and arrange the tomato slices over the top, placing them very close together. Scatter the cheese over the tomato slices, and bake for about 30 minutes, until the top is golden brown and the inside lightly set.

RIGATONI, LEEK AND RICOTTA CHEESE BAKE Serves ❹

INGREDIENTS

1 pound leeks, trimmed and cut into ¼-inch slices

8 ounces rigatoni

salt

1 cup ricotta cheese

2 garlic cloves, peeled and crushed

½ cup sun-dried tomato paste

4 Tbs chopped parsley

⅓ cup pitted black olives, sliced

freshly ground black pepper

⅔ cup freshly grated
Parmesan cheese

Another handy dish that can be quickly put together ahead of time and baked later when you need it. A juicy tomato salad with some fresh basil, or roasted tomatoes done in the oven alongside the bake, complement it perfectly.

1 First fill a large saucepan with 4 quarts of water and bring to a boil over high heat for the pasta.

2 Set the oven to 400°F. Grease a casserole dish or roasting pan about 8 x 12 inches and at least 2½ inches deep.

3 Meanwhile, cook the leeks in a little boiling water for about 6 minutes until they are tender, then drain them.

4 When the water in the saucepan boils, add the pasta along with a tablespoon of salt and give the pasta a quick stir. Briefly put the lid on until it starts to lift, showing that the water has come back to a boil, then let the pasta bubble away, uncovered, for about 8 minutes, or until it is tender but still has some bite to it.

5 Drain the pasta, return it to its pan and mix with the leeks, ricotta, garlic, sun-dried tomato paste, parsley, olives and salt and pepper to taste.

6 Spoon the mixture into the prepared dish, scatter the Parmesan cheese on top and bake the pasta for about 30 minutes, or until golden brown.

BELL PEPPERS STUFFED WITH PASTA, TOMATO, OLIVES AND CHEESE Serves ❹ as a main course, ❽ as an appetizer

You could use golden or green bell peppers equally as well as red ones for this dish, or, if you're making enough for a crowd, use a mixture of all three peppers for a particularly colorful effect.

1 First fill a saucepan with 2 quarts of water and bring to a boil over high heat for the pasta.

2 Set the oven to 400°F. Grease a casserole dish or roasting pan large enough to hold the halved peppers in a single layer.

3 When the water in the saucepan boils, add the pasta along with a tablespoon of salt and give the pasta a quick stir. Briefly put the lid on until it starts to lift, showing that the water has come back to a boil, then let the pasta bubble away, uncovered, for about 8 minutes, or until it is tender but still has some bite to it.

4 Meanwhile, heat the oil in a medium-sized saucepan and put in the onion; cover and sauté for 5 minutes. Then add the mushrooms and garlic and cook, uncovered, for a further 5 minutes, until the onion and mushrooms are tender.

5 Drain the pasta and add to the mushroom and onion mixture, along with the béchamel sauce, tomatoes, olives, cheese and salt and pepper to taste.

6 Put the bell peppers, cut-side up, in the baking dish or pan and fill them with the pasta mixture, piling it up well. Bake them for about 40 minutes, until the peppers are tender when pierced with the point of a knife and the filling is golden brown. Serve two pepper halves per person as a main course, with a crisp green salad, or put each half on a base of green leaves and serve to eight as an appetizer.

RICOTTA, CORN, BASIL AND PARMESAN CANNELLONI IN TOMATO SAUCE Serves ❹

INGREDIENTS

8 sheets of lasagne verde

salt

1 cup ricotta cheese

1½ cups canned corn, drained, or
1 cup fresh or frozen corn kernels

2 Tbs torn or chopped fresh
basil leaves

1⅓ cups freshly grated
Parmesan cheese

freshly ground black pepper

2 quantities of tomato sauce
(page 106)

Rather than use cannelloni tubes, which can be difficult to fill, I find it easier to use sheets of lasagne, cut in half, and wrapped around a filling, such as this mixture of ricotta, corn, basil and Parmesan.

1 Cook the lasagne in plenty of boiling, salted water for 6–8 minutes, or until tender but still with some bite. Drain and drape the lasagne sheets over the sides of the saucepan and a colander to prevent them from sticking together.

2 Set the oven to 400°F. Grease a casserole dish or roasting pan about 8 x 12 inches and at least 2½ inches deep.

3 Next, make the filling. Mix together the ricotta cheese, corn (no need to cook it first), basil and half the Parmesan. Season with salt and pepper.

4 Lay one of the sheets of lasagne out on a board; spoon a line of the filling down the long side of the sheet, then roll it up to enclose the filling and make a cannelloni roll. Cut the roll in half and place in the casserole dish. Repeat using the remaining lasagne and filling, making two layers of cannelloni.

5 Pour the tomato sauce over, scatter with the remaining Parmesan and bake for 35–40 minutes, until golden brown.

MUSHROOMS STUFFED WITH ORECCHIETTE, OLIVES AND CAPERS Serves ❹ as a main course, ❽ as an appetizer

INGREDIENTS

olive oil

1 onion, peeled and chopped

1 garlic clove, peeled and crushed

1 cup orecchiette

salt

⅔ cup béchamel sauce
(¼ of recipe on page 90)

4 sun-dried tomatoes, chopped

⅓ cup pitted black olives, sliced

2 Tbs capers

1 Tbs chopped fresh parsley

freshly ground black pepper

8 large flat mushrooms

⅓ cup freshly grated Parmesan cheese

This makes a piquant snack or appetizer.

1 Heat 1 tablespoon of olive oil in a medium-sized saucepan and put in the onion; cover and sauté for 5 minutes. Then add the garlic and cook, uncovered, for a further 5 minutes, until the onion is tender.

2 Fill a saucepan with 2 quarts of water and bring to a boil over high heat for the pasta. When the water in the saucepan boils, add the pasta along with a tablespoon of salt and give the pasta a quick stir. Briefly put the lid on until it starts to lift, showing that the water has come back to a boil, then let the pasta bubble away, uncovered, for about 8 minutes, or until it is tender but still has some bite to it.

3 Drain the pasta and add to the onion mixture, along with the béchamel sauce, sun-dried tomatoes, olives, capers, parsley and salt and pepper to taste. Keep warm.

4 Wipe the mushrooms and trim the stalks so that they are level with the black gills. Brush the mushrooms lightly with olive oil, season with salt and pepper and place, black side up, on a broiler pan. Place under a hot broiler for 3–5 minutes, to partially cook them. Remove from the heat, but keep the broiler on.

5 Pile the stuffing mixture on top of the mushrooms, dividing it evenly, and scatter with the Parmesan. Place under a hot broiler for 5–10 minutes, until golden brown.

SPINACH AND RICOTTA CANNELLONI IN TOMATO SAUCE Serves ❹

INGREDIENTS

8 sheets of lasagne

salt

2 Tbs butter

1 pound frozen spinach, thawed, or fresh spinach, washed

½ cup ricotta cheese

1⅓ cups freshly grated Parmesan cheese

freshly ground black pepper

freshly grated nutmeg

2 quantities of tomato sauce (page 106)

This is excellent as either an appetizer or a main course. A salad of grated carrot, fennel and black olives goes well with it.

1 Cook the lasagne in plenty of boiling, salted water for 6–8 minutes, or until tender but still with some bite. Drain and drape the lasagne sheets over the sides of the saucepan and a colander to prevent them from sticking together.

2 Set the oven to 400°F. Grease a casserole dish or roasting pan about 8 x 12 inches and at least 2½ inches deep.

3 Next, make the filling. Melt the butter in a large saucepan and put in the spinach. Cook for 5–6 minutes, or until the spinach is tender, pushing it down into the pan and chopping it with the end of a metal spatula. Drain off any excess water, then add the ricotta cheese, half the Parmesan and a good seasoning of salt, pepper and nutmeg.

4 Lay one of the sheets of lasagne out on a board; spoon a line of the filling down the long side of the sheet, then roll it up to enclose the filling and make a cannelloni roll. Cut the roll in half and place in the casserole dish. Repeat using the remaining sheets of lasagne and filling, making two layers of cannelloni in the dish.

5 Pour the tomato sauce over the cannelloni in the casserole dish, scatter with the remaining Parmesan over the sauce and bake for 35–40 minutes, until the top is golden brown.

MUSHROOM CANNELLONI IN BÉCHAMEL SAUCE Serves ❹

INGREDIENTS

8 sheets of lasagne

salt

1 Tbs olive oil

2 Tbs butter

1½ pounds mushrooms,
cleaned and chopped

⅔ cup full-fat or low-fat garlic
and herb cream cheese

2 Tbs chopped fresh parsley

freshly ground black pepper

1 cup freshly grated
Parmesan cheese

1 quantity of béchamel sauce
(page 90)

You could use tomato sauce instead of béchamel for this dish if you prefer.

1 Cook the lasagne in plenty of boiling, salted water for 6–8 minutes, or until tender but still with some bite. Drain and drape the lasagne sheets over the sides of the saucepan and a colander to prevent them from sticking together.

2 Set the oven to 400°F. Grease a casserole dish or roasting pan about 8 x 12 inches and at least 2½ inches deep.

3 Next, make the filling. Heat the olive oil and butter in a saucepan, then add the mushrooms and sauté over quite a high heat for about 10 minutes or until tender and any liquid has boiled away. Remove from the heat and add the cream cheese, chopped parsley and salt and pepper to taste.

4 Lay one of the sheets of lasagne out on a board; spoon a line of the filling down the long side of the sheet, then roll it up to enclose the filling and make a cannelloni roll. Cut the roll in half and place in the casserole dish. Repeat using the remaining sheets of lasagne and filling, making two layers of cannelloni in the dish.

5 Add half of the Parmesan to the béchamel sauce, then pour the sauce over the cannelloni, scatter with the remaining Parmesan and bake for 35–40 minutes, until golden brown.

LEEK AND GOAT CHEESE CANNELLONI IN TOMATO SAUCE Serves ❹

INGREDIENTS

8 sheets of lasagne

salt

1½ pounds leeks, trimmed and
cut into ¼-inch slices

½ cup soft goat cheese

freshly ground black pepper

2 quantities of tomato sauce
(page 106)

⅓ cup freshly grated
Parmesan cheese

This is a good combination of flavors and colors – delicious with steamed broccoli.

1 Cook the lasagne in plenty of boiling, salted water for 6–8 minutes, or until tender but still with some bite. Drain and drape the lasagne sheets over the sides of the saucepan and a colander to prevent them from sticking together.

2 Set the oven to 400°F. Grease a casserole dish or roasting pan about 8 x 12 inches and at least 2½ inches deep.

3 Next, make the filling. Cook the leeks in a little boiling water until they are just tender: about 6 minutes. Drain, and combine with the goat cheese. Season with salt and pepper to taste.

4 Lay one of the sheets of lasagne out on a board; spoon a line of the filling down the long side of the sheet, then roll it up to enclose the filling and make a cannelloni roll. Cut the roll in half and place in the casserole dish. Repeat using the remaining sheets of lasagne and filling, making two layers of cannelloni in the dish.

5 Pour the tomato sauce over the cannelloni, scatter with the Parmesan and bake for 35–40 minutes, until golden brown.

STUFFED EGGPLANT SLICES WITH BÉCHAMEL Serves ❹

INGREDIENTS

2 medium-sized eggplants

salt

1 cup short pasta
(not macaroni)

olive oil

⅔ cup tomato sauce (½ of
recipe on page 106)

1 Tbs sun-dried tomato paste

2–3 good sprigs of basil, torn

freshly ground black pepper

1¼ cups béchamel sauce
(½ of recipe on page 90)

⅔ cup freshly grated
Parmesan cheese

Thick luscious slices of eggplant, sandwiched with a tasty mixture of pasta, basil and sun-dried tomatoes and baked in a béchamel sauce with a topping of Parmesan cheese, make this dish an excellent, substantial main course.

1 First cut a thin slice from each side of the eggplant: these will not be needed. Then cut each eggplant downward so that you have four thick slices from each one. Put the slices into a colander, sprinkle with salt and leave for an hour to draw out any bitter juices and also to prevent the eggplant from absorbing too much oil when you fry it. Then rinse the eggplant slices under cold running water and squeeze it dry.

2 Fill a saucepan with 2 quarts of water and bring to a boil over high heat for the pasta.

3 Set the oven to 400°F. Grease a casserole dish or roasting pan large enough to take four eggplant slices in a single layer.

4 When the water in the saucepan boils, add the pasta along with a tablespoon of salt and give the pasta a quick stir. Briefly put the lid on until it starts to lift, showing that the water has come back to a boil, then let the pasta bubble away, uncovered, for about 8 minutes, or until it is tender but still has some bite to it.

5 Meanwhile, fry the eggplant slices in a little olive oil, on both sides, until tender and lightly browned. Or brush them on both sides with olive oil and broil until tender.

6 Drain the pasta, return to the still-warm pan and add the tomato sauce, sun-dried tomato paste, basil and salt and pepper.

7 Put four slices of eggplant in the baking dish or pan. Top each with the pasta mixture, dividing it evenly between them, then top each with another slice of eggplant. Spoon the béchamel sauce over the top of the eggplant "sandwiches," scatter with Parmesan cheese and bake for about 30 minutes, until golden brown.

Index